100

THINGS TO DO IN
OHIO'S
AMISH COUNTRY
BEFORE YOU
DIE

Enjoy Amish country!

Brandy Gleason

100

THINGS TO DO IN
OHIO'S
AMISH COUNTRY
BEFORE YOU
DIE

• •

BRANDY GLEASON

REEDY PRESS

Library of Congress Control Number: 2021950834

ISBN: 9781681063713

Design by Jill Halpin

Printed in the United States of America
22 23 24 25 26   5 4 3 2 1

We (the publisher and the author) have done our best to provide the most accurate
information available when this book was completed. However, we make no warranty,
guaranty or promise about the accuracy, completeness or currency of the information
provided, and we expressly disclaim all warranties, express or implied. Please note
that attractions, company names, addresses, websites, and phone numbers are subject
to change or closure, and this is outside of our control. We are not responsible for any
loss, damage, injury, or inconvenience that may occur due to the use of this book. When
exploring new destinations, please do your homework before you go. You are responsible
for your own safety and health when using this book.

• •

DEDICATION

To my husband, Matt, who supports my crazy. He has always given me free rein to explore and plan trips on a whim. Thank you for being my chauffeur and security team. I promise to try and be a better navigator, but I will still always blame Siri.

CONTENTS

• •

• •

Sports and Recreation

Culture and History

• •

• •

PREFACE

As a child raised in a conservative Mennonite home, I have always been drawn to Ohio's Amish Country. It has felt like an extension of home to me. The beautiful countryside, rolling hills, and friendly people have held my heart and attention since I can remember. As a little girl, Ohio's Amish Country was a place where I could go and enjoy a slower pace of life. I loved seeing the simple ways and playing with my Amish and Mennonite friends. Sitting by the side of the road and watching the buggies fly by, listening to the clip-clop of the hooves hitting the pavement, and lying back in the grass watching the clouds are highlights of my childhood. Amish auctions were something I looked forward to with rapt anticipation, hearing the auctioneer's song as he took bids for beautiful quilts and handmade furniture.

Amish Country has changed a bit since I was a little girl; there are more people visiting and the towns are busier and a tad more touristy, but the core of Ohio's Amish Country has stayed the same. Sundays are still the Sabbath here, and most of the stores and restaurants are closed. As the community has grown, so have the Amish Districts to encompass the Old Order, New Order, and the New New Order. Mennonites have expanded to add some churches where there are no head coverings worn, but the tenets of the faith remain strong. Choose your adventures here wisely; you will find the pace of life slow, but the time you have here will fly by.

• •

While picking out only 100 of the best places to explore and experience in Ohio's Amish Country was a challenge, it had to be done. I hope you find this book to be a springboard to enjoying everything Amish Country has to offer. Millersburg, Berlin, and all the other small towns along the routes will welcome you with warm hellos, and unique finds are around every bend in the scenic road. Enjoy one of the places in America where family is still important, food brings people together, and harmony and peace are the heartbeat of the community.

Things to know
- Don't take pictures of the Amish.
- Drive with caution around the backroads, and watch for buggies and bikes.
- Buy a copy of the *Budget*, America's first Facebook.
- Always check hours before heading to a store or museum; most have varied hours and are seasonal.
- Bring cash. Most Amish stores do not accept credit cards.
- Almost everything is closed on Sunday.

• •

ACKNOWLEDGMENTS

To my eight children, who let me grade all their papers growing up, and who ate hot dogs and cold cereal while I wrote; to my parents, who always have been my biggest cheerleaders and told me that one day I would be a writer; to Sara Broers with Midwest Travel Network, who encouraged me to write more—she was a catalyst; and to Shannon Carter with the Holmes County Chamber of Commerce and all the other community partners. Without these people in my life enjoying each adventure, finding places to explore, and sharing their knowledge, I couldn't have written this book.

SOUP & SALAD

Homemade Soups ... Cup 3.49 Bowl 4.99
Chili, Vegetable Beef, Chicken Noodle or Soup of the Day.

Amish Door Salad Bar 🅐🅳

More than 50 delicious choices fresh from our kitchen, including our Famous Graham Cracker Pudding.

(Cold Bar Only)
All You Can Eat............................. 10.99
Those sharing will be charged full price.

SANDWICHES

Sandwiches include cup of soup or Fresh Cut French Fries.
Add Salad Bar for $4.99. Add American or Swiss cheese,
grilled onions or mushrooms, for .99 each. Add bacon 1.99
Add a beef patty for $2.49

Hamburger* 9.4⁹
Served on a grilled bun.

Cheeseburger* 9.5
American or Swiss Cheese served on a grilled bun.

FOOD AND DRINK

EAT WITH THE LOCALS
AT BOYD AND WURTHMANN

When you walk in the door to Boyd and Wurthmann you'll be hit with a permeating turn-of-twentieth-century nostalgia. If you ask anyone around this small but busy town, you'll get the same answer. "Not much has changed here in 85 years, and that is what keeps us coming back." Getting a seat here can sometimes be a challenge; don't be afraid to head to the original green countertop built in the 1940s with seating for nine and order a cup of coffee, which still only costs 99 cents a cup. While the decor doesn't change, the daily menu does; offers rotate with the seasons. The locally sourced peach pie, strawberry pie, and berry pies draw in locals and out-of-town visitors.

4819 E Main St., Berlin, OH 44610, 330-893-4000
boydandwurthmann.com

TIP
Always check the hours before you go; they change with the tourist seasons. Boyd and Wurthmann is closed on Sunday.

SERVE YOURSELF A PLATE
AT THE BUFFET

How do you find Mrs. Yoder's Kitchen? When you roll up to a four-way stop in what seems like the middle of nowhere in Holmes County, depending on the direction you come from, just look left or right, and you'll see it. Pull into the parking lot and head inside to wait for a table. Gaze around and take in the country charm; your focus will turn to the hot buffet. Mouthwatering side dishes ranging from homemade Amish noodles to bacon-infused green beans and freshly made mashed potatoes are waiting to fill your plate, but the crown jewel of this country-style buffet is Mrs. Yoder's special recipe, locally raised, hand-breaded, pressure-fried chicken. Owner Gloria Yoder is a local who treasures her community and serves up her love onto their plates every day but Sunday.

8101 State Rte. 241, Mt. Hope, OH 44660, 330-674-0922
mrsyoderskitchen.com

TIP
Mt. Hope is famous for its auction house, which is across the street. If a sale is going on, be prepared for a longer wait.

GET BRUNCH
IN A LOG CABIN

If you blink you might miss Rebecca's Bistro, because it looks like a house and not a restaurant. However, once you know about this place, you'll never pass by again without stopping. The quaint ambiance of the inside cabin and homey decor welcome you, but it is the food that will bring you back. Farm-to-fork ingredients are at the heart of everything that comes out of the kitchen, and the table is regularly graced with supersized sandwiches, soups of the day, or one of the daily specials. If you fall head over heels in love, you can take home a bottle of her house-made salad dressing. To complete your experience, finish off your meal with a colossal slice of cake, gluten-free scones, or a decadent specialty coffee before you say goodbye.

4986 Walnut St., Walnut Creek, OH 44687, 330-893-2668
rebeccasbistro.com

TIP
Parking can be challenging; I recommend coming early in the morning or after 1:30 p.m., but don't wait too long—they close at 3 p.m.

DRESS UP FOR DINNER
IN THE WOODS

In an area known for homey comfort food, Tarragon is a delectable find on a woodsy off-road in the middle of Amish Country. When walking in, the captivating aura takes you to another level. The food mirrors an upscale menu that could be found in New York City. The executive chef will specially prepare each entrée and then make his way around to your table to ensure you enjoy every bite of his divine creations. Seasonally, Tarragon modifies the menu with local flavors grown locally. It is said that the executive chef prepares "classic food that is intentionally prepared with a delicate hand." Don't miss this one-of-a-kind dining experience that's off the beaten path and in the middle of nature.

6920 County Rd. 203, Millersburg, OH 44654, 330-674-0011
innathoneyrun.com/dining

TIP
Make a reservation before you go and if you want to linger, stay in a honeycomb suite at the Inn at Honey Run, where the rooms are built right into the rolling hills.

SIP YOUR WAY
THROUGH AMISH COUNTRY

Enjoy an evening at one of the local wineries peppered through the countryside and *wine* down while watching the Amish buggies head home for the night. Each winery has a unique flavor and style, and each has a signature wine. Creating an atmosphere of peaceful relaxation, the wineries bring community and friends together. Just outside of Sugarcreek, Breitenbach Wine Cellars features a laid-back outdoor patio with stunning hillside views. Experience a restored turn-of-the-century mill in Baltic, where guests at Baltic Mill Winery can drink in the rustic charm. In Loudonville, one of the most uniquely named wineries, The Ugly Bunny, can't be missed. Dine here in the evenings at their full restaurant and enjoy the picturesque setting, delightful wines, and brisk hard ciders. Amish Country's rich fertile soil and rolling hills help produce full-bodied wines that are among Ohio's best and create an atmosphere perfect for enjoying them.

Breitenbach Winery
5934 Old Rte. 39 NW, Dover, OH 44622, 330-347-3603
breitenbachwine.com

Ugly Bunny Winery
16104 OH-39, Loudonville, OH 44842, 419-994-0587
uglybunnywinery.wpcomstaging.com

Baltic Mill Winery
111 E Main St., Baltic, OH 43804, 330-365-0524
balticmillwinery.com

INDULGE IN SHERBET
LIKE NEVER BEFORE

Go ahead, indulge in some first-rate homemade soft serve sherbet. Jump in line at one of the three Miller Creamery locations and try some local favorites. This family-owned operation was born when Norman Miller decided he was ready to make a lifestyle change and leave the corporate world behind. Starting in a small food trailer on a small leased patch of land, the first summer open they realized they needed to make this a year-round venture. Now with Miller Creamery in fixed locations year-round, guests can enjoy the sweet treat anytime. Find specialty sherbet flavors that vary at each location and try them all! And if the sherbet is not enough, grab some small-batch caramel corn made just how grandma used to do it.

Original location: Open April–September
1706 E High Ave., New Philadelphia, OH 44663

Dover location: Open year-round
211 W 3rd St., Dover, OH 44622

Millersburg location: Open year-round
105 W Jackson St., Millersburg, OH 44654, 234-301-9004

millerscreamery.com

TIP

If you can't make up your mind,
the local favorites are Black Raspberry
and Prickly Pear.

DRINK CRAFT BEER
WITH THE WOOLY PIGS

Head out to the countryside to grab a pint with the wooly pigs at Wooly Pig Farm Brewery. While you're here for the brews, the pigs are a welcome addition to your evening on the farm. Kevin and Jael Ely are the connoisseurs, brewmasters, and brains behind this beer-and-farm venture. This crazy family-run enterprise began after a work trip to Bavaria, where they fell in love with Bavarian-style brews. Get a Rustic Helles, a classic light German beer suitable for the beer snobs and craft beer newbies alike; but watch out, because it goes down easy. While there is no restaurant on-site, on most weekends from March to October you can find a food truck or just bring your own pizza! Wooly Pig is family-friendly, dog welcoming, and the perfect spot for an authentic brewery farm experience.

But why wooly pigs? That's a story that is best told over a beer; ask a family member as they walk by.

23631 TR 167, Fresno, OH 43824
woolypigfarmbrewery.com

SUPPORT BUILDING COMMUNITY

In a tiny community on the edge of Holmes County, you'll find East Main Kitchen. Locals rave about it, but if someone didn't tell you about this off-the-beaten-path restaurant, you'd never even know it was there. Famed for serving comfort food with a modern twist, their first-class chef turns out some of the most divine plates found anywhere. East Main Kitchen's story has its beginnings in a meeting several years ago when a local church was looking for ways to interact with the community of Baltic in a more meaningful way. In 2017, with the encouragement of the Baltic mayor, the church purchased a building on the main street and started to support the neighborhood through fantastic food. Gather around one of their tables to indulge in their take on Shrimp and Grits, a specialty coffee, or a piece of their mile-high, multilayered scrumptious cake.

108 E Main St., Baltic, OH 43804, 330-897-9065
eastmainkitchen.com

SAMPLE SWEETS
FROM LOCAL AUTHENTIC BAKERIES

No one will need to tell you twice to head out to one of the many Amish bakeries; they will automatically draw you in with the smell of freshly baked sweets and loaves of bread. Don't ask for recipes, because most places make delectable treats the way they have been made for hundreds of years. They are family secrets! Kauffman's Bakery uses their Grandma Lili's baking methods to fill their shelves with German potato bread, Bavarian filled cream sticks, and sweet rolls. Miller's Bakery, known for its scrumptious tartlets, treats visitors to a genuine Amish welcome. Shop the small attached store for locally made crafts and extraordinary hand-sewn items. Have you ever seen a donut the size of your head? If not, take a trip to Amish Country Donuts for a glazed donut experience you won't soon forget; it's so big you might think about sharing it.

TIP
Pace yourself when stopping in at these bakeries. Don't go hungry, and make sure to take some home for later.

Kauffman's Bakery
(Open Sunday)
4357 US 62, Millersburg, OH 44654
330-893-2129
kauffmanscountrybakery.com

Miller's Bakery
4250 Township Hwy. 356
Millersburg, OH 44654

Amish Country Donuts
522 Dover Rd. NE, Sugarcreek, OH 44681
330-852-5214
amishcountrydonuts.com

STEP INTO A 1937 BARN
FOR AN ALL-YOU-CAN-EAT EXPERIENCE

In Smithville you can find yourself dining at The Barn, built in 1937 by the Imhoffs. Large, hand-hewn wooden beams, rustic antiques, and days-gone-by ambiance fill The Barn, which is known for its all-you-can-eat salad bar housed in a converted antique farm wagon. Stuff yourself with every imaginable topping, succulent coleslaw, and orange fluff dessert. But that's not all; among the sides are five different soups, including chili, cream of broccoli, and vegetable beef, and five different kinds of homemade bread. Don't finish eating here without a piece of pie and ice cream à la mode. Step outside The Barn and spend a minute enjoying the lake while feeding the geese and ducks. Also, just beyond the restaurant are "the shops," where you can get your shopping fix.

877 W Main St., Smithville, OH 44677, 330-669-2555
thebarnrest.com

TIP

You can still see the builder's signature and construction date on the southwest wall. Ask a server to show you where.

SAMPLE FARM-TO-FORK SPECIALTY FLAVORS

Why try a pizza place in an area known for comfort foods? Because you've never had pizza quite like this before. Good food starts with the best ingredients, and Park Street Pizza takes the blue ribbon for pizza pie done right. They call their suppliers their friends, and most everything you put in your mouth here is locally sourced and homegrown. With that thought in mind, it is no surprise that for every season there are new menus where they add ingredients to create superb seasonal collections. From fresh greenhouse-grown greens, plump heirloom tomatoes, or farm-fresh meats, everything is simply perfect. The Park Street Deluxe has an ideal blend of their most popular toppings! A classic house-made red sauce, nitrate-free pepperoni, mushrooms, organic Italian sausage, green peppers, red onions, and hot banana peppers will tantalize your taste buds. Stop in for one of the specialty pizzas and enjoy your slice of life!

215 R Dover Rd. NW, Sugarcreek, OH 44681, 330-852-2993
parkstreetpizza.com

SEE PANORAMIC VIEWS
FROM THE WALL-TO-WALL WINDOWS

Holmes County is home to rolling hills and lush valleys, and the Der Dutchman in Walnut Creek offers the best restaurant views around. With such a gorgeous panorama and some of the most delicious Amish fried chicken to be found, the place can be hopping. In peak season, you'll want to get in line well before lunch or dinner to snag one of the prime tables and avoid the line that can go out the door and down the wrap around porch, but don't worry if you're late—it moves fast. Der Dutchman was started by a local Amish man named Albert Hershberger in 1967, but due to the growth and the need for electricity, it was sold in 1969. It was purchased by a local family group that continues to invite you to join in the tradition of gathering around the table to share a warm meal with close family, dear friends, and significant others.

4967 Walnut St., Walnut Creek, OH 44687, 330-893-2981
dhgroup.com/restaurants/der-dutchman-walnut-creek-oh

TIP

Stay next door at the Carlisle Inn of Walnut Creek—book a room with a balcony overlooking the beautiful farm scenes of Mudd Valley. In the fall during harvest season, the views are particularly stunning.

RECHARGE
AT LOCAL COFFEE SHOPS

Coffee lovers will be in heaven in Ohio's Amish Country, because this community loves their java (and their tea). Spread out over the small villages and towns are lots of places serving up good, strong coffee or a variety of specialty drinks. He Brews Coffee is a play on the title of the book of Hebrews from the Bible, and its mission is to bring the love of God to the people through coffee and fellowship. Wallhouse Coffee, located in the heart of Little Switzerland, serves what they consider the finest coffee in the world. Drink flights have taken America by storm, and Tulipan Hungarian Pastry and Coffee Shop has embraced them. Order a flight of some of their specialty coffees and pair it with a Hungarian Tea Cake or Bishop Hat. The Red Mug Coffee is everything you're looking for in one spot: artisan coffee and small-batch roasted coffee right on the property. It is a coffee lover's dream.

He Brews Coffee Shreve
104 S Market St., Shreve, OH 44676
330-789-1036
shrevehebrews.com

Wallhouse Coffee Company
751 Dover Rd. NE, Sugarcreek, OH 44681
330-852-6209
wallhousecoffee.com

Tulipan Hungarian Pastry and Coffee Shop
122 S Market St., Wooster, OH 44691
330-264-8094
tulipanwooster.com

The Red Mug Coffee
7789 County Rd. 77, Millersburg, OH 44654
330-775-2880
theredmugcoffeecompany.com

DINE IN A HISTORIC BUILDING
ON THE FARM

It is no surprise that you find farm-to-table fare at Malabar Farm Restaurant. If you know anything about Louis Bromfield, the original owner of this land, you know he would be proud of the care and thought that goes into preparing the food before it graces the tables at Malabar. Farm to table means everything is sourced responsibly and grown locally. Elegant tables fill the historic home with the simple flicker of a candle as the centerpiece. Bite into sumptuous filet mignon, succulent lamb chops, or a fresh garden salad with house-made dressing from the chef. Experiencing fine dining in the countryside of Malabar Farm is a truly unbeatable dining event.

3645 Pleasant Valley Rd., Lucas, OH 44843, 419-938-5205
themalabarfarmrestaurant.com

TIP
Next door to the restaurant is the old spring house and farm stand location where the Bromfield's used to sell their produce. Read the signs and enjoy the peace of the farm.

FIND THE SPIRIT OF MOHICAN
FOR A DINNER LIKE NO OTHER

To make a night out with friends even more enjoyable, try doing it in a restored historic building in the heart of Loudonville, Ohio. Nothing like this hip casual joint has ever opened in this small but thriving town, and locals can't seem to get enough of it. High-end, refined dishes come out in rapid succession as the front door swings to and fro, filling up the dining room. The Black Fork Bistro is known for killer burgers, delicious pizzas, and the famous Black Fork Sundae—a colossal scoop of vanilla ice cream served over a dark chocolate brownie, with caramel sauce and candied pecans—no one leaves this place hungry. It is not unusual to find that everyone in Amish Country cares about the community, and each visionary brings something unique to the table. The spirit of Mohican is alive in well at the Black Fork Bistro.

153 W Main St., Loudonville, OH 44842, 419-920-9019
blackforkbistro.com

OPEN THE DOOR
TO A MEAL YOU WON'T FORGET

Enter into a place that approaches perfection when you open the door at The Amish Door in Wilmot, Ohio. Delicious smells of home cooking fill the senses and draw one to the table for a good long look at the menu. The "made from scratch" offerings are what bring people back over and over to this country destination: succulent fried chicken, golden brown loaves of fresh bread, a 40-item salad bar, and the famous buggy trail sundae! Don't come without calling ahead to reserve the authentic Amish Buggy that seats five to dine in. The plush buggy seats will give you an idea of what Amish transportation feels like without being out on the road. Even if you don't feel hungry when coming here, you will be as soon as you smell the welcoming aroma.

1210 Winesburg St., Wilmot, OH 44689, 330-359-5464
amishdoor.com

TIP

There is more than a restaurant here; the complex has a 52-room homey hotel with an indoor pool and the Shops at The Amish Door. Guests don't even need to leave to find all the Amish Country treasures.

DINE IN THE BASEMENT
OF KIDRON TOWN AND COUNTRY

When you walk into Kidron Town and Country and start to look for the restaurant, it might take you a minute to find it . . . at least it did for me. A staircase at the back of the Amish-style grocery store leads you down to the store's basement. As you reach the bottom of the steps you enter a small shoe store, and to the left is the restaurant. You are greeted by an old-school U-shaped counter with stools where you belly up to choose from some of their comfort fare. Choose from a quarter-pound hamburger, or one you can barely fit into your mouth. Or opt for farm-fresh fried chicken or some of the ham loaf made right in the grocery's meat department. Some say that this is where the Amish actually eat, and truth be told, you might be the only Englisher in the place when you come. That means the food is good!

4959 Kidron Rd., Kidron, OH 44636, 330-857-2131
kidrontownandcountry.com

TIP
From a trusted local source, the peanut butter cream pie here is the best around.

TRY A TASTY ORIGINAL
HOT TRAIL BOLOGNA TREAT

Troyer's Trail Bologna is out in the middle of nowhere, but they have been around for what seems like forever. Since 1912 the Troyer family has made these smoked, delightful rings of trail bologna in Trail, Ohio. The building where they welcome you has been there since 1932; it is a rebuild, because the original location burned down. It is like stepping back in time when you thrust the door open and step onto the creaky wooden floors. Service here is fast, and you will have your wax paper-wrapped sandwich in hand before you can count to three. The menu is simple, but you can choose your toppings for your trail bologna sandwich, including your choice of American, Swiss, or hot pepper cheese. Sit at the counter or walk to the porch and dangle your feet off the side and watch the Amish buggies clip-clop by as you enjoy the #1 sandwich in Holmes County.

6552 OH-515, Dundee, OH 44624, 330-893-2414
troyerstrail.com

BUNDLE UP AND EAT
WHERE YOU BUY YOUR CHRISTMAS TREE

Put on your red toboggan, climb aboard the Pine Tree Caboose, and tromp through the snow around the 150-acre Christmas tree farm to pick out your festive tree. After your adventure on the farm, bring the rosy-cheeked family in to have lunch at The Granary at Pine Tree Farm. The Granary is open year-round; however, there is something special about the gift barn at Christmas time, when it is decorated to the hilt. Fill your table with steaming cups of hot chocolate, delicious quiche du jour, their famous French onion soup, and a plate full of their sinfully delicious lemon crumb muffins. Sit back and enjoy the scenery through the wall of windows overlooking the lakes and snow-covered pine trees.

4374 Shreve Rd., Wooster, OH 44691, 330-264-1014
pinetreebarn.com/dining/gourmet-dining

TIP
The Granary at Pine Tree Barn is only open during lunchtime, and they are always busy because of their fantastic gourmet meals; reservations are highly recommended.

IMBIBE
AT HOLMES COUNTY'S ONLY BREWERY

Raise a glass at Millersburg Brewing Company, where the locals gather to enjoy the locally brewed beer. All brews are made in-house, and the owners will tell you they love what they do. Everything is made in the basement of a 1920s building, and the view from your high top table of all the goodness is a highlight you don't want to miss. With over 21 beers on tap, you don't need to worry whether they will have something to tempt you. Whether you prefer fruity flavors, ales, or IPs, your beer-loving taste buds will be thanking you. Millersburg Brewing Company isn't just about beer; they have a full menu. Delight yourself with Bavarian Pretzel sticks served with house-made beer cheese, Buffalo Cauliflower, or one of their specialty flatbread pizzas.

60 E Jackson St., Millersburg, OH 44654, 330-674-4728
millersburgbrewing.com

TIP
Holmes County is not a dry county, but two of the main townships where the Amish live are still dry.

PETER
PUMPKIN

LARGEST PUMPKIN EVER ON THE FARM

WEIGHS 760 LBS

Hershberger's
FARM & BAKERY LTD.

MUSIC
AND ENTERTAINMENT

ENJOY LIFE ON THE FARM
AT HERSHBERGER'S FARM AND BAKERY

Hershberger's Farm and Bakery is home to hundreds of farm animals, a farmers market, and Amish-run food stalls. When you roll up to the farm, the goats will greet you from the top of the large barn. When the car door swings open, the sounds of the cocky rooster, mooing cows, and the Big Boy draft horse will get you all kinds of excited. Don't miss the petting zoo, where you can buy feed and carrots to give the farm animals. These guys are quick, so hold on tight to the fodder, or one just might eat everything you have in 2.2 seconds. Buy a ticket to take an Amish buggy ride around the farm. The farmers market, where they sell literal piles of local produce and some of the best fry pies in the world, can't be missed. Plan for a half-day in this fully immersive farm experience.

5452 State Rte. 557, Millersburg, OH 44654, 330-674-6096
hershbergersfarmandbakery.com

WALK IN THE FOOTSTEPS
OF AMERICAN HEROES

Dennison Railroad Depot Museum is recognized as a National Historic Landmark and is one of the last remaining examples of a US railroad canteen that reflects a World War II heritage destination. What makes the heritage of this fully restored station so poignant? During WWII, 1.3 million service members were served free food by 4,000 working volunteers from the Dennison Depot Salvation Army Servicemen's Canteen. As the trainful of service members rolled into Dennison, they were scared, hungry, and about to be sent off to war. As they disembarked, the Salvation Army met them with sandwiches and drinks, bringing smiles and hope to these all-American boys. Dennison's name became Dreamsville, Ohio, to these men, and you can listen to the song made famous by the Glenn Miller Band. Inside the museum, you can find encased in glass a sandwich wrapper that a serviceman carried in his wallet through the whole war and kept until his death, confirming to us all how vital the canteen was.

400 Center St., Dennison, OH 44621, 740-922-6776
dennisondepot.org

LAUGH UNTIL YOU CRY

Every night at 5 p.m., they roll up the sidewalks and close up shop in Amish Country. Finding something to do might be a challenge; however, you can take an evening for some knee-slapping, side cramping, family-friendly fun at the award-winning Amish Country Theater variety show. This hilarious show will have you crying as "the Beachy's" sing their parody songs and crack some corny Amish jokes, while Lynard will have you rolling on the floor with his insane antics. Grab some munchies from the on-site snack bar; in true Amish fashion, almost everything is homemade. Throughout the year, they present special guests and shows that bring in top acts and tributes from every genre of music. You'll find the variety show located in the Schrock's Heritage Village complex in a state-of-the-art facility tucked off the road.

4365 State Rte. 39, Berlin, OH 44610, 888-988-7469
amishcountrytheater.com

TIP

Stay at the Encore Hotel, conveniently located next door, for discounted tickets and first-rate access.

SING
WITH AN AUCTIONEER

Give me two dollars, two . . . who, who, who will give me two? During the summer months, the Amish and Mennonite community come together to have benefit auctions for overseas missions, healthcare for those ailing in their churches (Amish do not usually have health insurance), Amish Country one-room schools, and the local civil service departments. What you will find at one of these shindigs are local handcrafted furniture, stunning hand-sewn quilts, and all that home-cooked food that people from all over the world have come to enjoy. It's quite a thing to meander through the auction, being shoulder to shoulder with all the Amish men, women, and children. "Jah! Vat?" Can be heard from them as they chatter in their Pennsylvania Dutch dialect. Make room in the car to take home some of the auction finds because things go at a "right gut price! Jah!"

TIP
Visit any restaurant or store and look at the bulletin boards as you enter; this is where they post signs and information about the local Amish auctions.

VISIT
AN "AMISH WAL-MART"

No one can resist visiting these "bent and dent/salvage" locations once they know about them. They're commonly called "Amish Wal-Marts," and visitors can explore these oddities, which have shelves covered from floor to ceiling with returned, damaged, and almost out-of-date groceries. Treasures are hidden around each corner and under every pile. I snagged a weighted keyboard for $100.00 once! Grocery surplus stores are a little more organized than the bent-and-dent ones; check dates before buying, because some things can be pretty old. Allot plenty of time to explore for hidden treasure; you'll want to dig in for a bit. These Amish-owned stores are usually right next to the Amish homestead and are typical of what you will find through all of the Amish Country; shining gas lamps and skylights are present to let in the light, and wood or coal stoves provide heat in the wintertime.

TIP
Call before you go, because Amish oddities can have different hours
and days they are open.

Brookside Surplus
2949 SR 93, Sugarcreek, OH 44681
330-852-4528

Country Salvage Bent-n-Dent Groceries
9420 Kidron Rd., Applecreek, OH 44606

Route 62 Bent-N-Dent Discount Groceries
1297 SR 67, Wilmot, OH 44689

Scenic Valley Surplus
10797 Kidron Rd., Fredericksburg, OH 44627

WATCH CHEESE BEING MADE

There's something quite thrilling as you pull open the doors to the Swiss-themed Heini's Cheese Chalet. Heini's has been a staple in the area since 1935 and has been turning out cheese ever since. Swiss-born Peter Dauwalder was the mastermind behind the creation of this cheese conglomerate, and he got even more creative with his cheese production as he began welcoming visitors. Making people smile as they sampled dozens of his unique cheeses inspired him to continue. Since Peter's passing in 2020 his family has continued the family traditions of making award-winning cheese, welcoming guests as if they were family, and sharing their love of their Swiss heritage. You can still enjoy watching them make cheese and take one of their tours when visiting; call ahead for that week's cheese-making days.

6605 County Rd. 77, Millersburg, OH 44654, 330-893-2131
bunkerhillcheese

TIP

Make sure to visit early in the day; Heini's can become busy in the late afternoons.

FEED THE ANIMALS BY HAND
ON AN AMISH HORSE-DRAWN WAGON

Line up and get ready to feed some animals that come from over six continents! From early springtime until October, The Farm at Walnut Creek welcomes guests to come and enjoy a day on their farm. Take a wagon or car ride through the farm, where you can hand-feed the giraffe, water buffalo, elk, deer, and even some camel! After your drive through the animal park, don't miss the family blacksmith shop and produce stand selling seasonal vegetables and fruits grown on their farm. Since you have been welcomed here, they invite you to tour their homes, the main house, and dawdy haus (grandparents' home). Gain a deeper understanding of how an Amish farm works and get up close to whatever they are working on for the day; it could be quilting, canning, or cooking up dinner for the family.

4147 County Rd. 411, Sugarcreek, OH 44681, 330-893-4200
thefarmatwalnutcreek.com

TIP
Bring plenty of cash, because they do not accept credit cards.

INHALE THE GOOD STUFF
AT A CHOCOLATE FACTORY

Everyone loves chocolate, and thanks to Coblentz Chocolates, folks can bite into this decadent treat in Amish Country every day. Signature offerings include classics like chocolate caramels, almond bark, buckeyes, and peanut clusters, which have been customer favorites since they opened in 1987. You're in the Buckeye State, so a buckeye purchase is a must. Once you bite into that peanut-filled center, you will be a buckeye fan—candy and football—for life. When visiting, you can often see the chocolates being made in the small factory behind glass in the viewing area. Each chocolate is meticulously scrutinized and checked before being approved. Create your own box of flavors of these handcrafted marvels—just ask for the box and fill it with whatever your heart desires, and if you want to ship some home, they can do that, too!

4917 Walnut St., Walnut Creek, OH 44687, 800-338-9341
coblentzchocolates.com

WATCH HISTORY UNFOLD
IN AN OUTDOOR THEATER

Trumpet in the Land is one of Ohio's premier and longest-running outdoor theater productions. This is a must-see for everyone interested in the rich history surrounding Amish Country. The drama brings to life the tragic but moving story of missionary David Zeisberger and his Christian Indian converts. Surrounded by the growing unrest of a nation being born and the coming of the Revolutionary War, David struggled to know what to do with his peaceful, nonviolent community of Shoenbrunne. *Trumpet in the Land* is brought to life in the same hills that this story unfolded in and poignantly shares the story. After the show, walk away with a deeper connection to how this peaceful people's influence affected the coming nation. Throughout the outdoor season, they also offer dramas and plays, like *The Sound of Music* and *Dracula*.

1600 Trumpet Dr. NE, New Philadelphia, OH 44663, 330-339-1132
trumpetintheland.com

TIP
Be sure to check the weather and plan your trip accordingly.

PICK FRUIT
RIGHT OFF THE TREES

When it comes to apple-picking in Homes County, it doesn't get any fresher than pulling one off the trees than at Hillcrest Orchard. Family owned and operated by the Merle Hershberger family, this 75-acre orchard produces 22 varieties of apples and 12 types of peaches. You'll want to bite right into one of their firm, sweet Evercrisps as soon as you hold it in your hand. Inside the family's beautiful warehouse, you won't just find apples. It's filled with local produce, locally made honey, and fresh-pressed apple cider that they make on site. In the fall, the store comes alive with everything associated with harvest season. Before you leave, walk out onto the balcony on the store's back to get a panoramic view of the gorgeous Mudd Valley.

2474 Township Rd. 444, Sugarcreek, OH 44681, 330-893-9906

TIP
This is a seasonal store and is open from August until March.

TAKE A DRIVE
DOWN MEMORY LANE

Since 1937 the Lynn Drive-In Movies' motto has been "Come as you are in the family car to see stars under the stars." Not much has changed since then except the movie stars themselves. The Lynn Drive-In is the oldest operating drive-in theater in Ohio, so it holds tightly onto its heritage of four generations. When you pull in, you'll notice not much has changed since its peak in the '30s; the audio still comes through the metal microphones that clip to your car. While they have kept the old school feeling, there have been significant updates to the digital projector and sound system, making a night out to one of the last grass drive-in theaters in the world a family memory. Rain or shine, warm or cold, you can come here to get your nostalgia fix as you watch a movie on the big screen eating lots of buttered popcorn.

9735 State Rte. 250 NW, Strausburg, OH 44860, 330-878-5797
lynndrivein.com

CATCH A FAMILY-FRIENDLY SHOW
AT DUTCH VALLEY

Every season at the Ohio Star Theater is an occasion to debut a new live Amish-themed musical onstage. Amish Country slows down in the evenings, but some guests are not ready to head to the hotel to read a book or watch TV. Night is when the stage at Ohio Star Theatre bursts into life with high-energy, unforgettable, family-friendly performances. Relax back into the padded chairs and be entertained with a story that will warm your heart and bring a smile to your face. Since opening its doors in 2017 with state-of-the-art lights and sound, the theater has been well received by the community and guests. Gather together to experience the featured seasonal show or one of their special events.

1387 Old State Rte. 39, Sugarcreek, OH, 855-344-7547
dhgroup.com/theatre

THROW AN AXE
IN AMISH COUNTRY

Need an activity in the evening while enjoying your stay? Hatchet Club in Sugarcreek has you covered. Hatchet throwing has exploded across the US, and carving out a niche in a new market can be challenging. However, the Hatchet Club has taken the experience to a new level. While many axe-throwing establishments offer a more rustic, bar-like environment, these folks have created a more refined, lounge-like experience to accompany the art of axe throwing. When you arrive for your reservation at Hatchet Club, you'll be introduced to your coach, who will give you a brief throwing lesson that includes proper grip, technique, and safety instructions. Your coach is then assigned to your lane for the evening to assist you and to help keep the jackaxes to a minimum. (*jackaxe (n)*: loud, disruptive thrower who doesn't respect his fellow axe throwers and may also toss back a few too many brews.)

528 McDonald Dr. E, Sugarcreek, OH 44681, 330-852-6042
hatchetclub.com

LIVE LIKE THE AMISH
FOR AN AFTERNOON

When traveling to Amish Country, you might be wondering about Amish daily life. Burning questions are always at the forefront of people's minds. Yoder's Amish Home takes guests on a detailed trip through a day in the life of an Amish family. In 1883, Johannes Hostetler built the barn on the property, and the cornerstone still remains with his name and the date inscribed. The dawdy haus, where the grandparents would have lived, is right next to the main house; you will be guided through both houses. One home is Old Order style, and the other is updated as a New Order Amish home. Go to school in the one-room schoolhouse to see how the teachers teach all eight grades at once. Amish buggy rides around the farm are a great way to top off this intriguing and educational stop.

6050 State Rte. 515, Millersburg, OH 44654, 330-893-2541
yodersamishhome.com

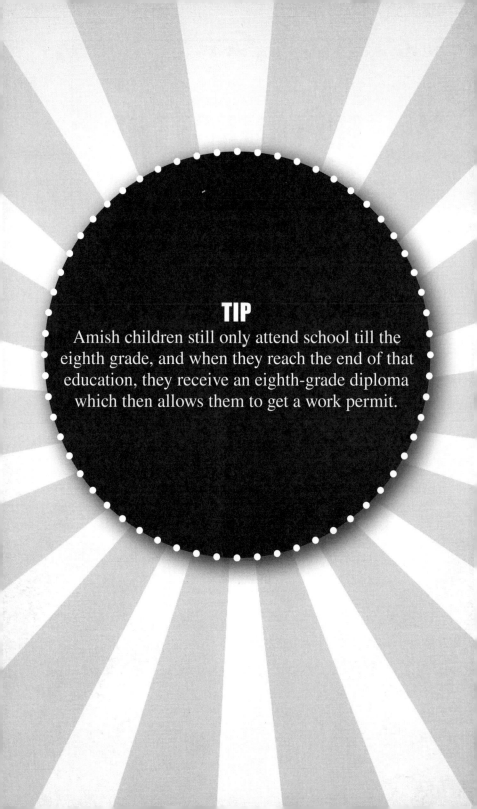

TIP

Amish children still only attend school till the eighth grade, and when they reach the end of that education, they receive an eighth-grade diploma which then allows them to get a work permit.

EXPERIENCE THE BACKROADS
ON AN AMISH TOUR

The backroads in Amish Country are full of stories, unknowns, and hidden places, and if you're here, you need to learn the lingo and insider knowledge. Rich Troyer, owner of Troyer's Amish Tours, is the man with the inside scoop. While on the tour, Rich, who was born and raised in Holmes County, takes his van loaded with tourists to all the unique places and shares his knowledge and love of the community. Learn the ways of the Amish, Old Order, New Order, and New New Order. Book the tour with the meal in an Amish home, where the Amish host, Edna Kline, serves the best dinner you will ever eat. Baked chicken, succulent creamed corn, brown buttered mashed potatoes, Amish noodles, homemade bread, and pies to die for are passed around the table family style. You'll come as a guest and leave as a friend.

Pickup location depends on where you are staying.
330-600-4948
troyersamishtours.com

FALL IN LOVE
WITH A CASTLE IN THE WOODS

Landoll's Mohican Castle, located in the densely wooded Mohican State Forest, creates a fairy-tale atmosphere of magic. It started as a dream in the heart of Army veteran Jim Landoll, who fell in love with European castles during his two-year stint in Europe. Here you will discover something right out of a child's storybook as you wander the exquisite, unique property. It is more than just a destination; it is an experience. Dine at The Copper Mug restaurant and bar, where you indulge in delicious fare fit for a king. Stay on the property in one of their specially designed rooms to enjoy the amenities and look for hidden treasures. There are guided tours of the property year-round, and if you visit during September and October, you can take a haunted tour of Heyd Cemetery and look for some of the spirits who call Landoll's Castle home.

561 Township Rd. 3352, Loudonville, OH 44842, 419-994-3427
landollsmohicancastle.com

LEARN THE LESSONS
LOUIS BROMFIELD TAUGHT US

Just who is Louis Bromfield, and what were his accomplishments? Born in Mansfield, Ohio, he would become a Pultizer Prize winner for his novel *Early Autumn*. Having lived for over a decade in France beginning in 1925, he recognized the looming danger as World War II approached, so he decided to move back to his roots to buy Malabar Farm. He was living out his dream, creating sustainable agriculture and championing conservation on his own back forty. Tour the home and outlying buildings and walk the halls where Humphrey Bogart and Lauren Bacall were married. Visit the educational center to learn about Louis's new ideas about farming. Malabar Farm State Park has made it their mission to keep Louis's legacy alive. This land that won the heart of Bromfield will win yours as well. Hike to the cave on the Butternut Squash trail, stay in the refurbished cabin on the pond, and in winter, come to see the sugar shack produce the rich amber maple syrup.

4050 Bromfield Rd., Lucas, OH 44843, 419-892-2784
malabarfarm.org

STAY TINY
IN A TINY HOUSE

Tiny houses have taken America by storm, and you can watch shows streaming on your devices about this culture shift to minimalism. However, before you take the leap into tiny living, you might just entertain yourself by staying in one of these custom-made creations. Hidden off the main road in the middle of Amish Country is a unique experience that will take you to your own personal Eden. A lighted path takes guests through the trees to a delightful grotto where you can sit by a fire or enter into your own private barrel sauna. After pausing and listening to the birds and watching the scurrying chipmunks, your eyes will turn toward the Scandi, the tiny house. While the house is small, every inch of space is maximized and each detail has been meticulously planned for your tiny experience. You'll love this little adventure so much that as you prepare to depart, you will be booking your next stay.

330-275-1744
tinystaysberlin.com

VOTE FOR WINNING RIBS AND BARBECUE

The Berlin Harvest Festival is an annual event held in September in Berlin, Ohio. This family-friendly event welcomes the best of the best for an event where the world's best pit masters battle it out for the coveted title of Rib Master. Stroll the sidewalks lined with vendors selling everything from handmade goods to freshly popped kettle corn. There are plenty of fun activities for kids as well. Taste some of the sumptuous ribs, vote for your favorite, and help one of the entrants win the People's Choice Award. Berlin Harvest Fest brings in live entertainment from local favorites to energize the crowd with foot-stopping music and comedy. Pause your day and find a seat on the sidewalk to watch the parade as it marches through town highlighting the local community. Bring a big bag to gather up all the candy, because the vendors and people are generous!

berlinharvestfestival.com

OTHER FESTIVALS

Ohio Swiss Festival
ohioswissfestival.com

Ohio's Amish Country Quilt Festival
ohiosamishcountryquiltfestival.net

Lehmen's Fall Festival
lehmans.com/storeevents

Great Mohican Pow-Wow
mohicanpowwow.com

Holmes County Antique Festival
holmescountyantiquefestival.org

Holmes County Fair
harvestridgeohio.com/holmes-county-fair

Music on the Square
Berlin, OH

SPORTS
AND RECREATION

LET YOUR IMAGINATION RUN WILD

Hidden among rolling hills and lush forest is a pathway leading you into a world of outdoor art. The Holmes County Open Air Art Museum, located at the Inn at Honey Run, will take you on a journey through the hillside and into a place where you are the master of interpretation. Each art installation is created by artists who share their passion for creation in an outdoor space. Enter through the *Primitive Gateways*, gaze at *Around the Bend*, which highlights the various colors of nature, or be mesmerized by *Archers Roost* floating above as you explore. But the one that stops guests in their tracks is *Being Time*, a grand structure of a cuckoo clock made primarily of organic material.

6920 County Rd. 203, Millersburg, OH 44654, 330-674-0011
innathoneyrun.com/open-air-art-museum

TIP
The Inn at Honey Run is an all-adult experience; children can come to the OAAM; however, use your discretion.

SWIM AND PLAY
AT AN INLAND LAKE

Since 1954, Baylor Beach Park has welcomed guests to enjoy fun in the sun at their water park and camping complex. It is owned and operated by the Baylor family, and the fourth generation proudly continues to create summer memories of outdoor merrymaking. What awaits you is a two-acre swimming lake that includes log rolls to test your balance, old-fashioned diving boards, and slippery water slides. Adjacent to the two-acre lake is a one-acre watersports lake where you can have a good time on kayaks or paddle boats. And there is more! Try finding glittering stones at the gem mining station or enjoy a friendly round of putt-putt in the evening. Before you head out, Baylor Beach's concession stand can tame anyone's hunger, so don't leave before grabbing a snack. If you want the fully immersive outdoor experience, bring along your travel trailer or tent and spend the night to continue relaxing by the flicker of a blazing campfire.

8777 Manchester Ave. SW, Navarre, OH 44662, 330-767-3031
baylorbeachpark.com

TIP
Baylor Beach water park is open from Memorial Day to Labor Day.

HORSE AROUND
THROUGH THE COUNTRYSIDE

Hop on the back of a regal horse with Amish Country Riding Stables and take a scenic ride through the rolling hills and lush trails in the heart of Amish Country. The gentle sway of the horse in the calm of nature highlights the stunning beauty of the surrounding landscape. Geared toward smaller and more intimate groups, this one-hour ride will be an experience you will never forget. Inexperienced? No worries; the skilled trail guides and friendly, steady horses can help you take on this new challenge, because there is no better way to make memories that will last a lifetime than on the back of a horse.

5025 OH-557, Millersburg, OH 44654, 330-893-3600
amishcountryridingstables.com

TIP

Amish Country Riding Stables welcomes riders ages eight years old and up for this unparalleled experience, and riders cannot weigh over 225 pounds.

GET YOUR GOLF GAME ON

Shout "FORE!" at one of Holmes County's stellar golf courses, where you can play on courses that have views for miles. The sloping greens in Amish Country will challenge your mental and physical game, but not enough to discourage you. Fire Ridge Golf Course has welcomed golfers since 1929 on their front nine holes featuring a more open course, and in 1999 the back nine, where the challenge of trees and blind tee shots are incorporated, were christened. Lodging and golf come together at the Black Diamond Course in Millersburg. The Lake House and Hackers Hideaway create an opportunity for families and friends to come to relax and experience the scenic and impressive course. Not only can you golf, but you can enjoy every amenity in these homes away from home. Both courses rent golf carts for the day, so there is no need to worry about dragging the gear around.

Fire Ridge Golf Course
1001 E Jackson St., Millersburg, OH 44654, 330-674-3921
fireridgegolfcourse.com

Black Diamond Golf Course
7500 Township Rd. 103, Millersburg, OH 44654, 330-674-6110
blackdiamondgolfcourse.com

ZIP THROUGH THE TREES

Calling all thrill-seekers and adrenaline junkies! Tree Frog Canopy Tours is for you. Spend the day in a canopy of trees at one of Ohio's premier zip-lining outfits. Meet your tree guide before your adventure and learn all the safety techniques, then clip on the safety harness and get ready to go from platform to platform with zips from 145 to 1,100 feet. This high-flying experience is not for the faint of heart; with seven zips, two sky bridges, and two rappels, be prepared to do a short uphill walk between zips after the first rappel, and then hang on tight as you whiz through the canopy, maneuvering the course. Groups with two well-trained guides take off at the top of every hour for the 2½- to 3-hour tour in the trees to give you the ride of your life through the Mohican forests.

21899 Wally Rd., Glenmont, OH 44628, 740-599-2662
treefrogcanopytours.com

IMMERSE YOURSELF
IN NATURE

Come out and play in the woods at the Wilderness Center, enjoying the nature playscapes. In today's world, phones, devices, and electronics have stolen time from young people and their desire to explore, so the Wilderness Center set out to create an outdoor space for young and old to get creative with organic material. Create a teepee with sticks, hop from log to log, or sit and spin awhile on the spider web net. After the outdoor play, visit the center itself to enjoy the exhibits of native Ohio animals and do some birdwatching from the bird viewing area. In the spring, the center blooms with some of the finest examples of Ohio's wildflowers. Before leaving, grab a t-shirt or handmade journal from the gift shop, where all the proceeds benefit the upkeep of the Wilderness Center and their ongoing conservation efforts within Ohio's Amish Country.

9877 Alabama Ave. SW, Wilmot, OH 44689, 330-359-5235
wildernesscenter.org

KAYAK AND PLAY
IN THE CANOE CAPITAL OF OHIO

It is not surprising that people come from all over the US to enjoy a day, week, or month at Mohican Adventures. This outdoor mega complex will keep adventurers busy with high-flying fun in the ariel park and family-friendly rounds of putt-putt. You can take a couple of laps around the family race track made for ages 10 and up, and they have created the fast and furious slick track for ages 16 and up. Mohican Adventures is well known for its floats down the Mohican River. Families, couples, and solo travelers can rent kayaks, canoes, rafts, or tubes to make their way downstream, where they pick you up. After a day of play, stay at their fantastic campground in one of their premier cabins or campsites, where a whole new level of outdoor adventure can be added.

Mohican Adventures
3045 State Rte. 3 S, Loudonville, OH 44842, 419-994-2267

Canoe Livery and Fun Center
419-994-4097

Campground
mohicanadventures.com

BIKE ON
AN AMISH BUGGY PATH

It might surprise you to learn that travelers can rent an e-bike to cycle the Holmes County Rails to Trails with Charged Ride e-bikes. For a small fee, you can have the e-bike delivered at one of the trailheads, your preferred lodging, or at the Mt. Hope store. What is an e-bike? Really, e-bikes are just bikes. What makes them unique is a small electric motor that can give you either a gentle boost or enough power to conquer almost any hill. You'll be able to make the 20-mile round trip to Killbuck or the shorter 10-mile round trip to Fredericksburg without a hitch. As you bike the path, you'll encounter Amish buggies using it for a quick and safe way to get where they are headed. The clip-clop of the hooves and smiling kids hanging out the back of the buggy makes for a gregarious ride.

306 S Millersburg St., Holmesville, OH 44633, 330-600-2984
chargedride.com

EXPLORE ONE OF OHIO'S STATE PARKS

Mohican State Park and Mohican-Memorial Forest are a nature lover's dream. With thousands of acres to explore and find adventure, you might never want to leave. Clear Fork Gorge, Lyon's Falls, and the Mohican State Scenic River are just a few of the must-sees for adventurers. Each hiking trail in the park is semi-improved and maintained by the state parks system. Walk through the dense vegetation, scurry across footbridges, stroll among the stately Hemlocks, and stay and ponder awhile at Big Lyons Falls; every part of these trails is magical. Stop at Mohican State Park Lodge to dine in Bromfield's Dining Room for some seasonal fare. Within the parks, stop to reflect at the Mohican-Memorial shrine honoring Ohioans killed in World War II, the Korean War, the Vietnam War, the Persian Gulf War, and the Afghanistan and Iraq wars. Mohican-Memorial Shrine is the state's official monument to honor nearly 20,000 sons and daughters who died during those conflicts.

TIP
Book a room or cabin a Mohican State Park Lodge; it's the perfect basecamp for Ohio's Amish Country.

Mohican State Park
3116 State Rte. 3, Loudonville, OH 44842
ohiodnr.gov

Mohican State Park Lodge
4700 Goon Rd., Perrysville, OH 44864
419-938-5411
mohicanlodge.com

Mohican-Memorial Shrine
950 ODNR Mohican Rd. 60
Perrysville, OH 44864
419-938-6222
ohiodnr.gov/wps/portal/gov/odnr/go-and-do/
plan-a-visit/find-a-property/
mohicanmemorial-shrine

GO CHASING WATERFALLS

Who knew Amish Country had waterfalls? While you are probably here for the food, it's nice to be able to walk off those fry pies and extra dips of ice cream. Honey Run Waterfall is a short hike from the gravel parking lot. The path is dotted with lush greenery, with a dirt trail leading down to the falls. Water cascades across the face of the rocks into a delightful pool of sparkling water. Ditch your shoes and soak your feet. Dundee Falls, located in Beach City Wildlife Area, is a 15-foot cascading fall that should have consistent water falling any time of the year. This trail is considered easy and takes you down to the falls quickly. Both of these hikes are pleasant and accessible at any time of the year. Waterfall chasing is the perfect way to stop to refresh and reset.

Dundee Falls
8525 Dundee Wilmot Rd. NW, Dundee, OH 44624

Honey Run Falls
10855 Hazel Dell Rd., Howard, OH 43208, 740-392-7275
knoxcountyparks.org/parks/honey-run-waterfall

PUTT-PUTT
A HOLE IN ONE

It's no surprise that on Sunday visitors are looking for things to do. Country Acres Mini Golf is the new kid on the block and is open all week long from April to October—yes, even on Sunday. Inspired by their Granma Keeler and her uncanny ability to entertain the grandkids on putt-putt outings, the owners of Country Acres decided to create a place where others could make family-friendly memories. There are two courses of play: the barn or the bridge. Each course is 18 holes. The barn course was created with family in mind, with plenty of opportunities for holes-in-one. This moderately challenging course will keep the family entertained with water features, an Ohio barn, and a fascinating windmill. While it is not considered ADA or stroller compatible, they say the barn course is mostly wheelchair and stroller friendly. If you're up for the challenge, take on the bridge course. With 18 challenging holes, this experience will test the best of putt-putters! A roaming water feature, significant elevation changes, a covered bridge, and unexpected obstacles will keep everyone on their toes.

4367 State Rte. 39, Berlin, OH 44610, 330-449-9986
countryacresminigolf.com

WALK
IN A QUIET GARDEN

Clary Gardens, located in Coshocton County, brings all the beautiful things to life. The gardens are open year-round and it is easy to see why nature and flower lovers come here. Enjoy a walk through the woodsy nature trails to stop and smell the roses in the rose garden. Spread out over the property, and find special, quiet places to reconnect with nature and oneself. Overlooking the property are the stately 1830s Compton house, the 1850s office building, and the beautiful springhouse. Open the wooden gate at the springhouse to step into a magical secret garden, close your eyes, and listen to the soft, sweet sounds of running water. Walk around the estate to get a feel for the history that permeates the home. Visit while they are hosting one of their programs or educational events to learn more about the flora and fauna of Ohio.

588 W Chestnut St., Coshocton, OH 43812
clarygardens.org

TIP
Bring the kids to the storybook walk, which will take them on a delightful walk through nature as they read a book.

THROW
SOME CLAY BIRDS

If you walk through the shopping areas of Amish Country, you will see women smiling and walking as fast as they can from shop to shop. One of the owners of Airport Ridge Sporting Clays said, "Behind every happy woman, you see a man slowly plodding along behind her with his head down and bored to death. Our goal is to entertain him here." And entertain him they will! With state-of-the-art atlas throwers located at 30 stations throughout the course, there is a station for every skill level. Shooting sports are like golf with a shotgun, and are among the fastest-growing sports in America. Rolling grasslands and densely wooded spots create a beautiful backdrop for your day out, yelling, "Pull!" While shooting is a male-dominated sport, it is no surprise that women love this course as well. Rent a shotgun or bring your own; don't worry if you forgot anything, because they have you covered.

9537 County Rd. 292, Millersburg, OH 44654, 330-674-2777
airportridgesportingclays.com

EXPERIENCE
A BIT OF HOLLYWOOD

Fans of *The Shawshank Redemption* can take a self-guided driving tour of 15 filming locations throughout North Central Ohio. Start wherever you like on the driving trail and end where you want as you drive to see the sites at your own pace! The closest spot to start in Amish Country is at Malabar Farm State Park, and from that point you can move westward toward Mansfield. One must stop at the historic Ohio State Reformatory prison. This is a massive, stone structure where sightseers can walk the floors, hear the sounds of clanging steel, and feel the eerie aura of the paranormal that resides within the walls. Every stop along the trail is unique. From green space, historic buildings, woodworking shops to pawn and antique shops along the way, The Shawshank Trail was created for people who love the movie and want to have an immersive experience; it is a one-of-a-kind movie encounter.

The Shawshank Driving Trail
shawshanktrail.com

BE A BIRDER
AT MILLER MANOR

Standing high on a hill overlooking Mudd Valley is a five-bedroom brick Georgian manor that birders from across the USA can rent. This estate can sleep 16+ people for a night or a week to explore Holmes County and the birds that can be found there. With the rental of the Manor, guests get access to 25 acres where birders can bird-watch during their stay in Amish Country. Birds that bring guests are yellow warblers, brown thrashers, chimney swifts, and Baltimore orioles, along with over 50 other identified species. Miller Manor is not only perfect for birding but a spacious and spectacular place to experience Amish Country's sensational sunrises and sunsets from the front porch and back balcony.

2606 State Rte. 39, Sugarcreek, OH 44681, 330-893-3636
dhgroup.com/inns/miller-manor

TIP
Guests who stay here are put in touch with a local Amish man who can take them on bird-watching tours on the property for a fully mesmerizing bird-watching experience.

MAKE A SPLASH
ON THE WATER

Take a day or two and enjoy the water at Pleasant Hill Marina, part of the Muskingum Watershed Conservancy District. With a plethora of things to do, you'll find yourself immersed in outdoor adventure fit for any activity level. Pleasant Hill Marina is known for its high-speed fun. Boaters can kick it into high gear while waterskiing, tubing, or just enjoying the fast ride. Rent a boat, wave runner, kayak, or stand-up paddleboard to maximize your time on the lake. Kids and adults can get out on the Whoa Zone, a floating island of slips, slides, and climbs at the sandy beach. Gather your group together to hike the plentiful trails that crisscross the park and seek out the osprey and eagles that inhabit the trees along the water. Finish out your time at the water in one of the deluxe log cabins hanging out in one of the hot tubs on the deck, watching the sun go down.

3431 State Rte. 95, Perrysville, OH 44864, 419-938-7884
pleasanthillpark.mwcd.org

BATE YOUR BREATH
AND HOLD ON TIGHT

Catch a rodeo at Buckin' Ohio and experience the Western way of life in Ohio. With a vision and a dream, Eileen Thorsell pioneered agritourism by taking her working ranch and using it to create one of the only facilities that raise the bulls that are ridden in the rodeo held on property. When you walk onto the ranch, you will feel the spirit of America, the Wild West, the importance of family, and the power of hard work. Events hosted on the property are full of high-energy bull riding, fast and agile barrel racing, and mutton busting. Mutton busting is where little buckaroos ages five to nine are geared up to the hilt in Western wear and "cowboy up" for six exciting seconds trying to stay on a sheep. The crowd goes wild during this event to cheer on the kids. Buckin' Ohio has activities before each show, live western music, guided ranch tours, a fully stocked general store, and all the chuck wagon food you could ever dream of eating.

Buckin' Ohio
8154 Garman Rd., Burbank, OH 44214, 330-624-7205
buckinohio.com

FIND
OHIO'S SECOND-LONGEST COVERED BRIDGE

The Bridge of Dreams is Ohio's second-longest wooden covered bridge and the third-longest covered wooden bridge in the United States. In the 1990s, Knox County began acquiring old abandoned railways and converting them into multiuse trails. With a big dream and the tenacity to accomplish this project, the community came together to transform the 370-foot railroad bridge into a covered bridge. Skeptics said it could never be done, and the name Bridge of Dreams was born out of that thought. It is not unusual to have Amish buggies go flying by you on the 4.5-mile Mohican Valley Trail, since the Amish use the many multipurpose trails to travel throughout Amish Country.

16606 Hunter Rd., Brinkhaven, OH 43006, 740-392-7275
knoxcountyparks.org

TIP
Did you know there is a free bike lending program? This program is sponsored by Knox Public Health and Knox County Creating Healthy Communities. Danville Outdoors is a partner. The bicycles are provided by Knox Public Health, and Danville Outdoors stores the bicycles and handles the lending.

FUEL YOUR FOOTBALL PASSION

From its modest beginnings in 1963 to today, the Pro Football Hall of Fame has grown in both its size and in its standing in the world of football. Recognized worldwide as America's premier sports hall of fame, it welcomes visitors from all over the world every year. Don your favorite team jersey and take a day trip to Canton to experience the thrill of all things football. The Hall of Fame campus will engulf you with poignant information and stunning visuals, and the walk of fame will inspire guests to dream big. Complement your visit with a truly immersive and unique VIP Tour or Insiders Tour. One of the knowledgeable team members will guide you through the exhibits. You will gain deeper insight into the history of the game of football and a better understanding of the diversity of the presentations and collections.

2121 George Halas Dr. NW, Canton, OH 44708, 330-456-8207
profootballhof.com

TIP
Plan a trip during enshrinement week, when you can see the inducted hall of famers in one location.

BUILD A FIRE
FOR AN EVENING OF S'MORES

Camping is one of America's favorite recreational pastimes, and Amish Country has you covered with plenty of places to play, stay, and explore. No matter what kind of camping you are looking for, whether tent, car, or RV camping, finding the right place to toast marshmallows and relax will be a snap. Campgrounds in Amish Country can offer plentiful fishing lakes, fun-filled kid areas with indoor and outdoor pools, jumping pillows, and various styles of campsites. No matter what your rig size is, one of the locations will have what you need, with most of the locations offering 50-amp service, full hook-ups, and all the amenities required for an evening campfire. You'll find yourself kicked back in your chair enjoying the sounds of nature after a full day exploring the Amish backroads.

TIP

Amish Country has curvy roads with lots of Amish buggies. Stick to the main routes to get to campgrounds; you'll be glad you did!

Amish Country Campsites
1930 US-62, Wilmot, OH 44689
330-359-5226
amishcountrycampsites.com

Scenic Hills RV Park
4483 Township Rd. 367, Millersburg, OH 44654
330-893-3258
scenichillsrvpark.com

Berlin RV Park
5898 SR 39, Millersburg, OH 44654
330-674-4774

Evergreen RV Park
16359 Dover Rd., Dundee, OH 44624
330-359-2787
evergreenparkrvresort.com

Whispering Hills Jellystone Resort
8181 State Rte. 514, Big Prairie, OH 44611
330-567-2137
whisperinghillsjellystone.com

Coshocton KOA
25688 County Rd. 10, Coshocton, OH 43812
740-502-9245
koa.com/campgrounds/coshocton

CULTURE
AND HISTORY

LEARN THE HISTORIC ROOTS
OF THE PLAIN PEOPLE

Curiosity develops when exploring a culturally rich area, and Amish and Mennonite history is something every visitor to Amish Country should take time to immerse themselves in. Behalt, the Amish and Mennonite Heritage Center, takes you from the Anabaptist persecution in Europe to the settlement located here in Holmes County, Ohio, and everywhere in between. An Amish guide walks you through a 30-minute tour of the cyclorama painted by Heinz Gaugel. In 1962, Heinz came to Berlin and heard people talking in a German dialect similar to his own. He became fascinated with them, and in 1972 he moved here to paint the history of these plain people. The mission of Behalt is to accurately inform about the faith, culture, and lifestyle of the Amish, Mennonite, and Hutterites. Religion is at the heart of Amish and Mennonite culture, and they invite guests to know the Christ of their culture, His steadfast love, and His claim upon their lives.

5798 County Rd. 77, Millersburg, OH 44654, 330-893-3192
behalt.com

LISTEN FOR
THE STEAM WHISTLE
OF DAYS GONE BY

Every steam train lover must grace the doors of this stunning roundhouse in their lifetime. The Age of Steam Roundhouse is believed to be the only full-sized working roundhouse built since 1951. Stroll through the meticulously built, 18-stall, brick roundhouse surrounding a 115-foot turntable and pit, then gather around the tour guide to listen close, because they talk fast to get through as many of these mighty giants as they can. Stand by one of the massive wheels and look up toward the towering smokestack; you will feel small compared to the big black engines. Age of Steam spends hours, months, and even years restoring steam engines back to their rightful, stately place on the railroad tracks. Plan ahead when coming and book one of the specialty tours or events. These extended, more in-depth tours will fascinate and engage everyone, plus it gives you more time to look at each engine, watch the operation of the turntable, and see the restorations first hand.

213 Smokey Lane Rd. SW, Sugarcreek, OH 44681, 330-852-4676
ageofsteamroundhouse.org

WHITTLE ME
A PAIR OF PLIERS

The Ernest Warther Museum and Gardens takes people by surprise. Once they have been there, walked the grounds, examined the carved designs and trains, and heard the story, they tend to leave a little piece of their heart behind. "Mooney" Warther, master carver, artist, genius, and inventor, was the mastermind behind everything in the collection. His story is an interesting one: the youngest of five children, a found rusty knife, a second-grade education, and wooden pliers. It is notable that "Mooney" refused fame and fortune for his creations, though he was practically offered the moon for them. He chose a simple life of family and friends over the plaudits of the world. People came from all over the world through the years to see the man with the wild hair, loud booming voice, and genius mind who carved so intricately that you won't believe what he created until you see it for yourself.

331 Karl Ave., Dover, OH 44622, 330-505-6003
thewarthermuseum.com

EXPERIENCE ROSCOE VILLAGE:
AMERICA'S CANAL TOWN

The Ohio and Erie Canal brought travel and commerce to the new and growing state of Ohio. Little towns began to pop up along the canal, but as railroads and intercontinental travel became more accessible, the canal and their cities all but dried up. However, one town, historic Roscoe Village, has been restored and now welcomes people to remember the good old days. Take a self-guided tour featuring historic architecture and demonstrations of skills of the past, including blacksmithing, broom-making, and weaving. Visit the hands-on museum that gives kids of all ages the chance to try crafts such as tin punching and candle dipping. People come here for the history, but Roscoe Village is a town alive with unique shops lining the streets where you can satisfy your sweet tooth and buy local. The trip would not be complete without dining in one of the historic and architecturally rich buildings.

600 N Whitewoman St., Coshocton, OH 43812, 740-622-7644
roscoevillage.com

SLIDE ALONG THE OHIO-ERIE CANAL
ON A HORSE-DRAWN CANAL BOAT

Step onboard a fully reconstructed canal boat and take a ride through history with the *Monticello III* canal boat. Once you are seated on the *Monticello*, you can sit back on the wooden benches and think about what an 80-hour trip on something like this would have been like. Back in the 1800s, this trip would have been smooth and easy compared with the bouncing of a wagon or riding on horseback. Make sure to watch the hoggee (a towpath driver for the early 19th-century barge transportation system in parts of the eastern US) lead the huge team of draft horses as they pull the canal boat gently along its way. The *Monticello* canal boat ride deserves a spot on your Amish Country bucket list. The opportunity to take a 45- to 60-minute trip down a hand-dug canal on a replica canal boat is an uncommon treat.

23253 OH-83, Coshocton, OH 43812, 740-622-7644

TIP
Bring mosquito spray for the ride; the bugs want to make friends.

CHECK THE TIME
AT THE WORLD'S LARGEST
CUCKOO CLOCK

Sugarcreek is known as the "The Little Switzerland of Ohio," and moving this cuckoo clock—the largest in the world according to the *Guinness Book of World Records*—from its original home at the Alpine-Alpa restaurant in Wilmot to Sugarcreek's town center was a no-brainer. Built-in 1972, it stood for years on a hill in the back of the Swiss restaurant, where every 30 minutes, a three-foot-tall couple came out to dance the polka accompanied by Bavarian music and a five-piece Oompah band. When the restaurant closed the clock fell into disrepair until it was purchased by Walnut Creek Cheese, who donated it to the town of Sugarcreek. Volunteers worked to restore the cuckoo clock to its former glory, and it now continues to do what it was meant to do: chime in the hour and bring smiles to happy faces as they watch the twirling couple dance.

100 N Broadway St., Sugarcreek, OH 44681

TIP
The clock runs from 9 a.m. to 9 p.m. from April through November.

WALK THE STREETS
OF YESTERYEAR

Historic Zoar Village was founded in 1817 by a group of 200 German Separatists who wanted to escape religious persecution. Landing in Ohio, they built a community where they thrived for more than 80 years as a communal settlement. Today visitors can tour the town on foot and explore the buildings to learn more about the village. Your first stop is at the General Store and Visitors Center to purchase tickets and get your map. This store is distracting, because you will want to shop all the old-time goods. Book an in-depth tour with one of the guides for a well-rounded trip back in time. If the bakery is in operation the smell will lead you there, and seeing how they cooked for the whole community in one location might blow your mind. Round out your visit with a meal at the Canal Tavern of Zoar, which has been serving travelers on and off since 1829.

TIP
Zoar Village is open for tours April-October.

The Zoar Store & Visitor's Center
198 Main St., Zoar, OH 44697
330-874-3011
historiczoarvillage.com

Canal Tavern of Zoar
8806 Towpath Rd. NE, Bolivar, OH 44612
330-874-4444
canaltavernofzoar.com

EXPLORE THE REMAINS
OF A REVOLUTIONARY FORT

Fort Laurens is the site of Ohio's only Revolutionary War fort. Built in 1778 as a wilderness outpost, the fort served three purposes. Americans hoped to use the outpost as a base to attack the British in Detroit, deter the Native Americans loyal to the British from conducting raids on American settlers in Pennsylvania and Ohio, and finally offer protection for the neutral Christian Delaware who had settled at Shoenbrunne and Gnadenhutten. The fort was abandoned in 1779, and none of the fort remains above ground. However, on your visit you will see the outline of the fort, which is visible to the naked eye. During your tour, watch the short film to gain a greater understanding of the fort, the surrounding area, the role it played during the birth of America.

11067 Fort Laurens Rd. NW, Bolivar, OH 44612, 330-874-2059
fortlaurensmuseum.org

TIP
Plan to visit during June through August, because it is not open in the off-season.

PAY RESPECTS
AT GNADENHUTTEN

While this may not be the most uplifting stop, it should make it onto the bucket list. In 1779 missionary Rev. David Zeisberger founded Gnadenhutten to convert Delaware and Mohican Native Americans to Christianity. Those who converted lived at Gnadenhutten until the Revolutionary War, and in 1781 they were removed to the Upper Sandusky Area. In early 1782, some of the Native Americans returned to the area searching for food; sadly, they were met by Captain David Williamson and Pennsylvania militiamen. On March 8, 1782, the militia rounded up some 90 of the food-seekers, including women and children, and massacred them. Today there is a memorial for the lost and a place to pay your respects where the Native Americans are buried. Visit the small museum, but call ahead before going; the hours are sporadic. You can also walk the historic local cemetery. Considering the tragic story that was written here, there is a deep-rooted history that should always be remembered.

182 Cherry St., Gnadenhutten, OH 44629, 740-254-4143
traveltusc.com/directory/listing/gnadenhutten-museum-historical-park

---

TIP
Call ahead for museum hours because they can be random.

VISIT OHIO'S SETTLEMENT
OF FIRSTS

In 1772 a Moravian missionary named David Zeisberger came to the frontier of what would later become Ohio to convert the Native Americans living in what was considered a new land. Building Shoenbrunn as a pacifist community helped to bring a small space of neutrality in a land full of instability. As the village grew, the first church, first schoolhouse, and first code of laws were built and created in the new frontier. What happened to Shoenbrunn? Due to their pacifist stance on the impending Revolutionary War, Zeisberger ordered everything burned to the ground and moved the community. Today, you can visit the reconstructed log cabins and buildings and the cemetery and learn the fascinating history of the settlement. Walk the land where the beginnings of Ohio unfolded. Watch the introductory video, take your time walking the history-packed museum, and appreciate the tenacity of the people who came before us to tame the land in the west.

1984 E High Ave., New Philadelphia, OH 44663
ohiohistory.org/visit/museum-and-site-locator/schoenbrunn-village

SEE
THE FLEXIBLE FLYER SIDE CAR

Loudonville is a quaint town right on the outskirts of Holmes County, and a visit to the Cleo Redd Museum should make your list. Visitors can see an original Flxible Flyer sidecar that was manufactured from 1913 to about 1930. These were innovative for the time, and seeing one in person is impressive. Scientist and philanthropist Charles Kettering hails from the area, and Cleo Redd honors him with a room dedicated to his achievements. Among these are the electric starter, which eliminated the need for crank engines. Kids will love the mechanical village, and before leaving you can ask the curator to fire up the 1927 Reproduco player piano for some tunes from history. Walk across the street from the museum to explore the Workman Cabin, which was built in 1838 by Morgan Workman, a minister. It served as his home and as the church where he preached. Fun fact: it was inhabited by his family for nearly 100 years.

203 E Main St., Loudonville, OH 44842, 419-994-4050
crfmuseum.com

BE AMAZED
AT EXQUISITE DESIGNS

Seeing the carvings of David Warther is worth the trip to Ohio's Amish Country alone. If there is ever anything that will blow your mind it is watching this artist work right before your eyes. David Warther doesn't just carve—he creates. He is the grandson of Ernest Warther and has honed his craft since he was a child. The museum is laid out in a pristine and flowing fashion that will take you through the history of ships via intricate carvings from First Dynasty of Egypt to the present day. Guided tours are available. Scrimshaw, the art of engraving on ivory, is one thing you will see throughout the displays. It is achieved by scratching fine lines into a highly polished ivory surface and filling these scored lines with ink.

1775 State Rte. 39, Sugarcreek, OH 44681, 330-852-6096
warther.org

FEAST YOUR EYES
ON LOCAL ARTIFACTS

Killbuck Museum is the best-kept secret in Holmes County. It is tucked away off of the main roads; finding it without knowing about it would be a miracle. While this is a small six-room building, it is jam-packed with artifacts that you might expect to see in the Cleveland Museum of Natural History. Wander through cases of early Native American arrowheads, tomahawks, and other ancient items that will awe you. Many of the artifacts found in the Killbuck Museum were dug out from under rock shelters in the county. In 1993, a Mastodon was excavated, and the bones are on display. You'll find not only local history but a collection of rocks from around the world that will surely impress. The case with the fluorescent glowing rocks is an amazing addition to this rural historic gem. Room six is full of taxidermy, with over 150 specimens shot and collected from Northeast Ohio. Don't leave without seeing the remnants of the Duncan Mill and the two grinding stones imported from France.

Front St., Killbuck, OH 44637, by appointment: 330-763-0133

VIEW STUNNING CRAFTMANSHIP IN METALWORK
AT WENDALL AUGUST FORGE

Start your visit by watching the 10-minute video about the humble beginnings of Wendall August before checking out the forge. Craftsmen will come on occasion to share their art; however, the forge is currently not running on a daily basis. The tour is self-guided, and you can see how each piece of metal is handcrafted by their talented artisans. Ask for the Hammer Experience, which is free for all guests. You will be able to forge your own creation on one of the dies using a piece of metal and a hammer. Bring in a card available throughout Amish Country and receive a free ornament. If you are into finding quirky sites, the largest Amish Buggy in the World is located in the gift shop; take a selfie to share with your friends. Take home the forged nativity, one of the most popular items made to date.

7007 County Rd. 672, Millersburg, OH 44654, 866-354-5192
wendellaugust.com/ohio-amish-country-store

FIND ALL THE HISTORY
AT SMITHVILLE

Peppered throughout the area are historical societies preserving the rich culture and history of the region. Smithville Community Historical Society surprises visitors with its fully resorted Pioneer Village and working Mishler Weaving Mill. The Pioneer Village consists of Ivin Pioneer Cabin, Sheller House, the working village blacksmith, and the wheelwright shop, and docents and volunteers guide guests during special events. Summertime welcomes the hometown historic baseball team, the Smithville Stars, keeping the past alive for future generations. Christmas in the Village, one of the biggest events of the year, decks the Pioneer Village out with 1800s holiday finery. Interpreters in period dress sing jolly Christmas carols to the Schantz pump organ, and merrymakers roast marshmallows and drink cider while waiting to whisper in the ear of Old Saint Nick.

381 E Main St., Smithville, OH 44677, 330-669-9308
sohchs.org

TIP
The Mishler Mill has scheduled hours, and the Pioneer Village is only open on scheduled dates. Support the Society by purchasing one of the artfully designed rugs from the mill.

SEE A VICTORIAN HOME
IN ITS ORIGINAL STATE

In 1900 things were changing, and the Brightman family was making a move from Cleveland to Millersburg. In its day, this turn-of-the-century home was the epitome of all things new and innovative. Today, you can tour the 7,000-square-foot Victorian House Museum. In the basement you'll find the sauna, a wooden box with all the bells and whistles; the guides will tell you that you won't catch them using it. Throughout the home, there are still the original light fixtures that could be used with both electricity and gas. Right next door is the Millersburg Glass Museum, which houses the works of John Fenton. After checking out the glass museum you will want to hunt for some of this valuable glass at home or a thrift store; you might just be surprised at what you find.

484 Wooster Rd., Millersburg, OH 44654, 330-674-0022
holmeshistory.com/victorian-house

TIP
The Victorian House was highlighted on HGTV's production *Victorian America*.

JOURNEY
INTO HOLMES COUNTY'S GERMAN PAST

The German Culture Museum, while small in size, is big on history. This collection was gathered by two local men, Ed Schlabach and Wayne Hostetler, who went from auction to auction to collect items from the community with a long-term vision of someday sharing the artifacts in a museum that highlighted the people that made this community what it is today. Jonas "Der Weiss" Stutzman was the first settler to Holmes County, and one of the highlights at the museum is the 14 x 20 portrait of him dressed all in white. With a nod to the community's Christian heritage, the museum includes a small chapel where you will find intricately carved statues, imported from Germany, of the twelve apostles. While not a German piece, one of John D. Rockefeller's surreys in a fully restored condition is standing in the middle, which is a timeless treasure.

4877 Olde Pump St., Walnut Creek, OH 44687, 330-763-1390

TIP
Call ahead for hours, they change with the seasons.

RING THE SWISS BELLS
AT THE ALPINE HILLS MUSEUM

The Alpine Hills Museum, located in Sugarcreek, is known as the Little Switzerland of Ohio. Sugarcreek takes its Swiss heritage seriously, and the Alpine Hills Museum is the perfect place to learn more about the rich Swiss heritage of the region. View the 10-minute video before you start your tour, then push the buttons at the Swiss cheese-making exhibit and learn how the local cheesemakers created the 125-pound wheels of cheese; it is an arduous process. Visit the exhibit on the *Budget* newspaper, one of the longest-running print publications in the US; the locals like to call it the "Amish Facebook." You can buy a copy at many of the local stores.

Alpine Hills Museum
106 W Main St., Sugarcreek, OH 44681, 330-852-4113

Ohio Swiss Festival
ohioswissfestival.com

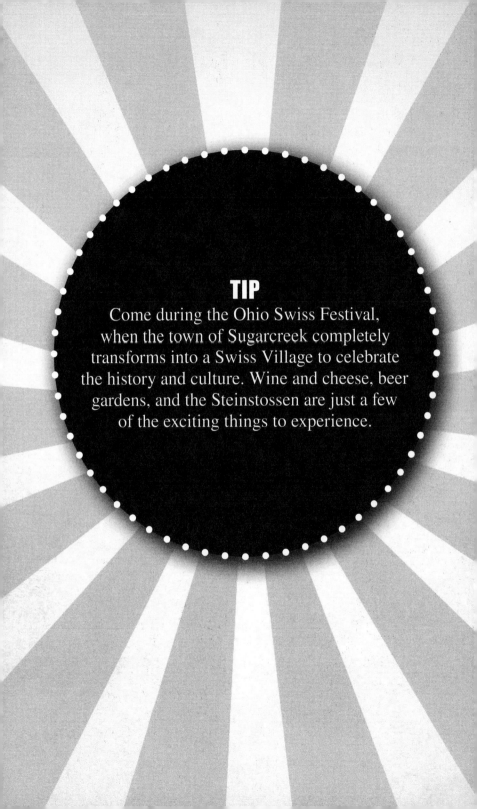

TIP
Come during the Ohio Swiss Festival, when the town of Sugarcreek completely transforms into a Swiss Village to celebrate the history and culture. Wine and cheese, beer gardens, and the Steinstossen are just a few of the exciting things to experience.

SHOPPING
AND FASHION

CELEBRATE CHRISTMAS
ANY TIME OF THE YEAR

The sounds of "White Christmas" echo through the doorway as you step into Tis the Season. Sights and sounds of holiday cheer are around every corner of this year-round Christmas extravaganza. The store specializes in every kind of Christmas decoration, and you can fill your home with specialty ornaments ranging from blown glass to handcrafted. Personalized ornaments fill one of the rooms, where Jill and Johnny can have their names placed on an ornament of their choice. The Hallelujah Chapel is filled with heavenly angels, from hand-sized to six feet tall; also found within the chapel are wooden benches where shoppers can sit and reflect on life or sing along with the Christmas music. Christmas trees abound throughout the store, so they have holiday merriment covered whether you want a Charlie Brown or massive 12-footer. Christmas lovers will be in heaven.

4363 State Rte. 39, Millersburg, OH 44654, 888-893-3604
tistheseasonchristmas.com

TIP
You can shop here until 6 p.m.—when other shops have closed, the Christmas magic continues.

FIND SOME TREASURES
AT THE WALNUT CREEK FLEA MARKET

Everyone loves to find treasures at flea markets. At the Walnut Creek Amish Flea Market, it's a shop until you drop experience, and it is all under one roof. Set upon a hill overlooking the valley, you'll find this gigantic complex full of all kinds of vendors. Wander through the stalls chock full of everything from rare antiques to Amish-made baskets and box store overstocks. Grandma Schrock's Kitchen will tempt your tummy with delicious food, ranging from snack goodies to gut-busting plates filled with sloppy joes or pulled pork. Don't be surprised if you hear over the loudspeaker about a giveaway in real time, because Amish Country loves its customers. Come during one of their special events like Eggstravaganza or the annual Chocolate Tour. Check the schedule for the live music events throughout the year; there is extra excitement in the air during these convivial weekends.

1900 OH-39, Sugarcreek, OH 44681, 330-852-0181
walnutcreekamishfleamarket.com

SEW
TO YOUR HEART'S CONTENT

If your motto is "Yes, I need more fabric," you are in the right place. Amish Country has a fabric shop in every small town and even off little dirt side roads. While many of these shops are here to serve the Amish community, it would be safe to say they are also dedicated to preserving the art of quilting and keeping the heritage alive. One won't just find fabrics in these country stores; stroll down aisles filled with sewing notions, items for embroidery and cross-stitching, and surprise finds of items from yesteryear. After securing a stack of fabric to take home, slow down to admire the handmade quilts adorning the racks in the store. Rich, vibrant colors intricately pieced together and then hand quilted with utmost care to create an exquisite piece of art that will inspire you to take your fabric and transform it into whatever you can dream.

Helping Hands Quilt Store
4818 State Rte. 39, Berlin, OH 44610
330-893-2233
helpinghandsquilts.com

Miller's Dry Goods
4500 OH-557, Millersburg, OH 44654
330-893-9899
millersdrygoods.com

Zincks Fabric Outlet
(huge with great discounts)
4568 OH-39, Millersburg, OH 44654
330-893-7225
zincksfabric.com

Lone Star Quilt Shoppe
7700 County Rd. 77, Millersburg, OH 44654
330-674-3858

CARVE A PERSONALIZED WOODEN CREATION

Some places will take you by surprise, and P. Graham Dunn is one of those places. When the sliding glass doors open, you are welcomed in like family, but the thing that will get you is the stunning woodwork and laser-engraved sign of the 10 Commandments. Peter Graham Dunn was the son of missionaries who served in China, and his passions were hard work, a loving family, and sharing Christ. His work continues today in the employee-owned stores. This 20,000-square-foot retail store will keep you entertained while shopping, and you'll want to take some time to watch the woodworkers creating laser-engraved items in their woodshop from the large windows on the upper level. Before you leave, visit the clearance bent-and-dent section for some significant savings.

P. Graham Dunn
630 Henry St., Dalton, OH 44618, 330-828-2105
pgrahamdunn.com

TIP
The grounds are stunning; pack a picnic to enjoy the lake and visit the small chapel to pause and reflect.

FIND EVERYTHING YOU NEED
TO MAKE A HOUSE A HOME

Keim is the best "lumber yard" in the Midwest; it is where tradition meets modern design. Since 1911 when it started with four employees to today's 700,000-square-foot complex, Keim will genuinely take your breath away. It was built as both a retail store and as a showstopper highlighting the exquisite quality they produce. Places like this can be dangerous for the budget, because you will want to buy unique woodworking products, choose something from the magnificent tool selection, and pick up some home décor items and gifts as well. Take a break from tool overload and climb the stairs to the Carpenter's Café, where you can put your feet up and have a piece of pie as you consider your purchases.

4465 OH-557, Charm, OH 44654, 330-893-2251
keimlumber.com

TIP
You can come here and explore even if you don't need woodworking items; it's the ultimate destination for a homeowner.

TAKE HOME AN HEIRLOOM

The craftsmanship of hardwood furniture in Amish Country has shoppers browsing in amazement. It doesn't matter what you are looking for to add to your home. The Amish woodworkers have it; you just have to find it. Driving the beautiful backroads brings furniture-seekers to many small, home-based shops and large buildings with elaborate displays housing these works of art. When coming to the small shops, walk in to find the craftsman creating exquisite master pieces—and he will get up straight from his workbench to greet you. While shopping, run your fingers over the glossy smooth surfaces of dressers, every size of bedroom set, elaborate dining room sets, and all the other things you can add to your house to make it a home.

TIP

You can order most anything, but be aware that there is usually a six- to eight-week wait for your piece of furniture since it is made to order and made by hand.

FURNITURE SHOPS

Country Furniture
4329 County Rd. 168, Millersburg, OH 44654
330-893-4455

Weaver Furniture
7011 State Rte. 39 NW, Sugarcreek, OH 44681
330-852-2701

Homestead Furniture
8233 State Rte. 241, Mt. Hope, OH 44660
866-674-4902
homestead-furniture.com

Brandywine Furniture
2482 Pyle Rd. NW, Dover, OH 44622
330-343-5224
thebrandywinefurniture.com

The Cabin Store
7860 State Rte. 241, Millersburg, OH 44654
330-674-1838

SHOP WHERE THE AMISH SHOP

Amish Variety Stores have an old-time feel with the gas lights burning, but also a gentle modern twist. Amish stores are located all over the five-county area, and taking some backroad adventures will have you coming up over one of the rolling hills to find a store in the middle of what seems like nowhere. Peek into the things that an Amish home needs. You never know what you will find, because each Amish district has different rules on guiding what they can have. Find that useful kitchen or farm tool you have been searching for, decorative home items, or a board game for a family game night back at your accommodations. Amish stores are the finds that make coming to Ohio's Amish Country magical and surprising.

North Market Variety
5603 Township Rd. 362, Millersburg, OH 44654, 330-893-4606

Housewares 77
6346 County Rd. 77, Millersburg, OH 44654

Ruby's Country General Store
2467 US-62, Dundee, OH 44624, 330-359-0406

TIP

Pack a cooler with ice for these backcountry moments, because these stores can have fantastic deals on meats and cheese.

EXPERIENCE ONE-STOP SHOPPING
IN A MEGA COMPLEX

Find everything people love about Amish Country in one spectacular location at Schrock's Heritage Village. Roll into a parking spot and prepare to enjoy an afternoon of shopping. Start your day at Berlin Pets, where you can hold and cuddle some puppies, and who doesn't love puppies? Then explore the Berlin Leather and Shoe, which is connected for some high-end western wear. Berlin Antique and Craft Malls hold thousands of hidden finds that grandma used to use and uniquely hand-crafted items made locally. The Plaid Sheep will help fill the craft basket, and you can shop for that little take-home item for the fabric lover. Take a peek behind the old screen door into Streb's General Store and find something to grace your table or a small souvenir of your time in Amish Country.

4363 State Rte. 39, Berlin, OH 44610, 330-893-3052
amishfarmvillage.com

TIP
The complex is also home to a large event center and Encore Hotel; it truly has everything you need in one place.

GATHER FRESH PRODUCE
FROM ROADSIDE STANDS

All throughout the main and backroads you will find farm market stands selling an abundance of local produce. Be on the lookout for small wooden or cardboard signs highlighting what is being sold on the farms. Sometimes the produce is piled up or displayed at the roadside, and at other times it is down the lane by the house. The colorful orange pumpkins, wagons full of corn, vine-ripened tomatoes, farm-fresh honey, and jars of amber-colored maple syrup are just some of the bounty found. If there is one time to go onto backroads, it is during harvest season to find excellently priced freshly harvested goods. Don't be shy; if there is a sign, it is a welcome from the farmer to come and shop.

TIP

Most of the time, you pay on the honor system at the Amish farms; make sure to bring small bills and coins to make change.

Blessings Acres
6719 Township Rd. 362
Millersburg, OH 44654

Troyer's Country Market
5201 CR 77, Millersburg, OH
330-893-3786
troyerscountrymarket.com

Miller's Farm Market
3460 State Rte. 39, Millersburg, OH 44654
330-893-2235

Walnut Creek Cheese
2641 State Rte. 39, Walnut Creek, OH 44687
330-852-2888
walnutcreekcheese.com

UNCOVER A HIDDEN CRAFT GEM

Sol's in Berlin was created for treasure seekers, those who like to unearth the one-of-a-kind unique, and DIYers. If you have the time, you can spend hours here exploring all three buildings packed full of everything a visitor to Holmes County could dream of finding. Yes, you read that correctly, three stores: Sol's Palace, Sol's Exchange, and Sol's Kit-N-Kaboodle. These are not just single-story stores either; some have three floors of shopping goodness. Find that gift for Great Aunt Helen (you know, the one who still pinches your cheek as an adult at Christmas time), something for the kids from the candy section, or a take-home for you! There is so much at Sol's that listing a few of the items you can find here would never do it justice; you have to go and see it for yourself.

4914 W Main St., Berlin, OH 44610, 330-893-3134
solsinberlin.com

TIP
Parking spaces in Berlin are scarce; park at Sol's to walk the downtown shops before returning to your car.

PROCURE A PIECE OF ART

Many don't think of art when they think of Holmes County; however, there is an art scene that will bring a sense of awe when you walk through the doors of New Towne Gallery in Millersburg, which brings together the finest in representational art and artisan work. Wander through the historic 1873 building and view art that represents the eastern frontier, 18th-century Colonial America, and the Woodland Native American Nations. Admire the handmade artisan goods, and period reproduction fine furniture. The gallery is the backdrop to many local events and a place that fosters authenticity, laughter, friendship, and faith. Want a piece of art for your home? Let your curiosity run wild, step back to admire, and imagine where these pieces would fit into your home.

55 W Jackson St., Millersburg, OH 44654, 330-473-6027
newtownegallery.com

LIGHT UP YOUR LIFE
WITH HEAVENLY SCENTS

Family owned and run by Amish sisters, Lamp and Light Candle Company is located just outside Walnut Creek, and it is a stop every candle lover needs to visit. Stepping into the store brings a sense of warmth and welcome as the Amish family greets you. They don't just sell candles; they share kindness, which in turn brings out the best in candle shopping. With old-fashioned skill and patience, these ladies hand-pour and hand-scent each and every candle that they sell. It's an art that has been slowly making a comeback in recent years. Don't be surprised by how many scents there are; just take your time, enjoy the fragrances, and pick your favorite. Call ahead and schedule to watch a demonstration of candle pouring or candle carving. Both events are interesting; however, the steady hand it takes to do the carving is incredible and mesmerizing.

4320 County Rd. 114, Sugarcreek, OH, 330-852-3234

DISCOVER SOMETHING BEAUTIFUL
AT SHEIYAH MARKET

Sheiyah means "barn" in Pennsylvania Dutch, and when the Schabach family rebranded their complex they wanted to bring a piece of their Amish culture and history together. It started as a small retail store in a bank barn which is now home to the Village Barn. Start your exploration at Buggy Brew with a cup of something warm to sip as you wander and get social at the #buggybrew buggies. Buggy Brew has two Amish buggies inside; you can sit in them and pretend to be Amish. The Gardens will delight you with decor and greenery for your home and outside. Sit a spell at the fire pits in the courtyard and snap a photo at the silo. Stylish, chic clothing will delight at the Sheiyah Style Boutique. At Christmastime, Sheiyah Market comes alive with holiday spirit, creating a magical shopping experience, and for the shopping queen this truly is the best time of the year!

4755 State Rte. 39, Millersburg, OH 44610, 330-893-2648
sheiyahmarket.com

DIG FOR BARGAINS
AND HELP THE WORLD

Everyone loves a good bargain, and Amish Country has plenty of thrift stores for you to find that one thing you have been looking for. Each of the thrift stores in Amish Country has a reason for being there; they are nonprofits supporting some kind of mission, which means that every dollar spent makes a world of difference. Shopping and helping others go hand in hand. When you purchase clothing, accessories, housewares, and more from the local thrift stores, you're both saving money and contributing to programs that help preserve and enrich lives. Each thrift store is unique and has its own style; however, they all have the plainclothes sections. This is where you can find Amish dresses, pants with buttons instead of zippers, and plain kids' clothes, which is a unique area for resale shops. What is one man's donation is another man's treasure.

THRIFT STORES

Save & Serve Thrift Store
1108 S Washington St.
Millersburg, OH 44654
330-674-1323
saveandserve.org

Trading Post Thrift Store
7703 State Rte. 241, Millersburg, OH 44654
330-674-1778
tradingpostthriftstore.org

Harvest Thrift Stores
1915 State Rte. 39, Sugarcreek, OH 44681
330-852-7467
harvestthriftstore.com

MCC Connections
4080 Kidron Rd., Kidron, OH 44636
330-857-7802
mccconnections.com

PEER THROUGH BINOCULARS
FOR BIRDING SUPPLIES

Birdwatching is one of America's favorite pastimes, and in Amish Country you will notice that the Plain People love their birds. Farms will have many birdfeeders around the homes, but what you really should be on the lookout for are their purple martin houses. Some properties might have a couple of houses, but many of them will have a village decked out with gourds. And as you might expect, there are plenty of places to find birding supplies, birdhouses, binoculars, and a wide variety of bird identification books. If you have fallen in love with those beautiful purple martins, you can purchase a Troyers Cedar T-14 purple martin house for your own backyard. Many of the stores are located on an Amish farm or a store on their property. Ask for some of their favorite birding tips, because these guys really know their stuff.

BECOME A HOMESTEADER
AT LEHMAN'S

Lehman's Hardware has been part of the Amish community since 1955. What started out as a small local shop has turned into a complex housing everything a homesteader and modern-day shopper would ever want or need. Carve out at least one or two hours for your trip back in time to explore every room and shelf filled with old-time goodies. While this is a mercantile filled with every imaginable thing a homesteader could dream of, they have incorporated a few hidden gems. The Museum of Light, featuring Aladdin Lamps, has almost every style of lamp ever made. Come hungry and enjoy a snack at Kidron Cast Iron Café, where you can regroup before heading in for more perusing. Local artist Paul Weaver's hand-carvings are showcased in Lehman's, and you can walk through the room dedicated to his like works. Lehman's stands for a simpler life, and no matter what season you are in on your journey, they have something for you.

4779 Kidron Rd., Dalton, OH 44618, 800-438-5346
lehmans.com

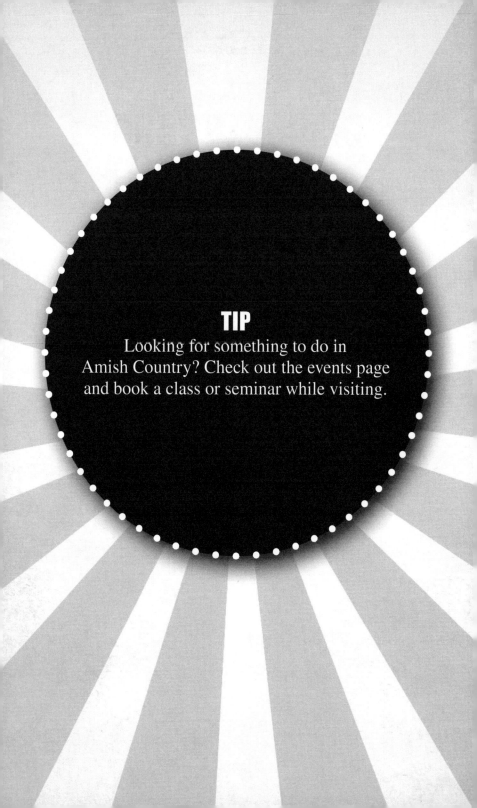

TIP

Looking for something to do in
Amish Country? Check out the events page
and book a class or seminar while visiting.

DISCOVER YOUR FAVORITE FLAVOR
AT THE J.M. SMUCKER CO. STORE

The J.M. Smucker Co. Store and Café welcomes you to a world of pure imagination. Your eyes will be immediately drawn to the back of the store to the rows of rainbow colors and the wall of history. Smucker's has been known for its jams and jellies, so shop that section first, grab your favorite, and stick it in your basket. Once you've got your coveted favorite, peacefully shop the rest of the brands. J.M. Smucker Co. Store is filled with all the good stuff, from peanut butter to coffee!

333 Wadsworth Rd., Orrville, OH 44667, 330-684-1500
jmsmucker.com/smucker-cafe-store

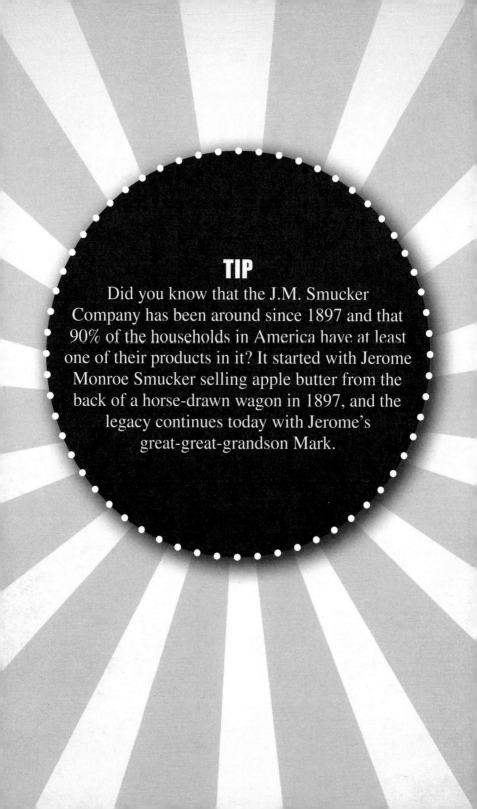

TIP

Did you know that the J.M. Smucker Company has been around since 1897 and that 90% of the households in America have at least one of their products in it? It started with Jerome Monroe Smucker selling apple butter from the back of a horse-drawn wagon in 1897, and the legacy continues today with Jerome's great-great-grandson Mark.

SCORE A VALUABLE FIND
IN ONE OF THE ANTIQUE STORES

Junkers, antiquers, and treasure seekers will be amazed at all the antique stores peppered throughout the Amish Country region. What you will find at one of these gems is nothing short of hidden treasure! Most of the stores are sectioned off by booths that are stocked by antique dealers that shop and live throughout the United States. This means you can find literally about anything your antique-loving heart desires. Let your imagination run wild as your hands run over these items of yesteryear. Who owned it? Where did it come from? These questions will probably never be answered, but it will become part of your family history when you buy it. Write down where you bought the piece, what you paid, and what it is, for future generations to enjoy. If you're looking for a memorable item to take home, the antique stores are the place to be. Bring cash, because many of the smaller and more obscure stops will not accept credit cards.

ANTIQUE STORES

Berlin Antique Mall
4379 State Rte. 39, Berlin, OH 44610
330-893-3051

Starlight Antiques
66 W Jackson St., Millersburg, OH 44654
330-674-5111
starlightantiques.com

Jackson Street Antiques
80 W Jackson St., Millersburg, OH 44654
330-674-0910
jacksonstreetantiques.com

Berlin Village Antique Mall
4774 US Hwy. 62, Millersburg, OH 44610
330-893-4100
berlinvam.com

Journey in Time
1314 Wadsworth Rd., Orrville, OH 44667
330-683-7503

Carlise Antiques
3205 State Rte. 39, Millersburg, OH 44654
330-473-7215

STOP AND SMELL THE ROSES

Amish are known for many things, but their flower and vegetable gardens aren't often mentioned. Stunning displays of deep reds, vibrant blues, and sunshine yellows grace the fronts of many Amish and Mennonite homes. Where do they get these healthy and beautiful plants? Amish greenhouses! A funny story from a tour guide was that they plant these tall and lovely flowers in the front of their gardens to hide the weeds. You are looking at the flowers, and you never notice the blemishes. Greenhouses are strewn all across the region, and from early spring to late fall, road-trippers can fill the car with all kinds of flower goodness. Springtime brings the annuals, vegetables, and perennial plants, and by fall, the hearty mums are in full bloom, ready for purchase. Many small greenhouses offer home-baked goods or have roadside vegetable stands next to the greenhouses; it is the ultimate in one-stop Amish shopping.

AMISH GREENHOUSES

Backyard Blooms
2998 County Rd. 200, Dundee, OH 44624
330-359-5195

Miller's Greenhouse
4150 County Rd. 160, Millersburg, OH 44654

Baskets and Blooms
5482 Township Rd. 629
Millersburg, OH 44654
330-893-3675

Mari's Flower Patch
2701 Township Rd. 410, Millersburg, OH 44654
330-390-0256

STROLL THE HISTORIC DOWNTOWNS
TO FIND EXCEPTIONAL BUYS

Amish Country offers many small villages with delightful historic downtowns. While these towns are not large, each has a unique feel. Millersburg has a haunted hotel, clothing made by Amish seamstresses at Farmhouse frocks, and the Holmes County Visitor Center. Berlin is known as the place to be, and most shops are accessible on foot—traffic can be congested here, and parking is limited. Visit the oldest building in town, Beeyond 1817. Wooster has the most extensive downtown, and you can spend hours shopping every block. You will be surprised at this kitschy, hip scene in the heart of the Amish. Round out your tour of downtowns shopping in Sugarcreek. The charming feel of "the Little Switzerland of Ohio" is welcoming, and plentiful shops will keep you busy for quite a while. This little burg offers the most diverse shopping, where you will find Swiss clocks, curio shops, and everything in between.

HISTORIC DOWNTOWNS

Millersburg
Berlin
Sugarcreek
Walnut Creek
Mount Hope
Wooster
Baltic
Charm
Wilmot
New Philadelphia
Loudonville

INDULGE IN THE WORLD OF POLISH POTTERY
AT OLD WORLD POLISH POTTERY

Twelve years ago, at a random auction, Roger Chenevey and his wife, Jennifer, bought a piece of Polish pottery. They began to wonder about the items they were eating off of and if they were safe, which led to research about pottery made in Poland. They purchased a few pieces to sell out on a roadside table, and people stopped to buy the beautiful works. That one piece of pottery eventually led to what you see here today at Old World Polish Pottery. Each piece is free of lead and cadmium, so they're perfectly safe to eat from. The pottery sold in this store is made in the small village of Boleslawiec, Poland, where skilled artists still individually handcraft and hand paint each piece using a hand-stamping technique and free-hand design. Each uniquely crafted item will entice the eyes, and a few might find their way into your hands to take home.

7110 Massillon Rd. SW, Navarre, OH 44662, 330-359-0185
oldworldpolishpottery.com

TIP
During the winter months, you have to call to make an appointment to come.

ORDER AWARD-WINNING MEATS
AT WINESBURG MEATS

Winesburg Meats has been family owned and operated since 1959, and they have been making quality products the whole time. While times have changed and equipment has been updated, the recipes have remained the same, and everything is still made without artificial preservatives, soy, fillers, or gluten. Push open the door to step back in time to be greeted by the family, who work the retail store every day. When a customer places an order, it is usually packaged by one of the sons, Anton and Taras, or the dad, Marion, who learned everything about the business from his father, Walter. Cases of coolers are filled with every imaginable kind of meat butchered in-house: every flavor of bratwurst imaginable, Winesburg Wieners (the best hot dogs in the whole world), hand-cut ribeye, and pork chops, to name a few; you name it, they probably have it. If you're looking for something to grill, smoke, or marinade, they've got you covered.

2181 US Hwy. 62, Winesburg, OH 44690, 330-359-5092
winesburg-meats.com

RENEW YOUR LOVE OF READING

If you are coming to Amish Country, you know there is a slower pace of life here among the rolling hills, especially during the evening. After five o'clock, everything around closes up, and people get comfortable wherever they have chosen to take lodging. For a small Amish community, you will find Christian bookstores in every small town and even on the backroads. Gospel Book Store in Berlin is the largest one in the area and has hundreds of books to choose from. Wander around the large selection of Bibles, Christian music, and religious gifts, and find the newest releases and oldies but goodies, too. If you stop at the Amish bookstores, you will find books written in English and German. Grab a copy of the *Ausbund*, the Amish hymnal, which has been around since around 1740. Many of the small stores have copies of books about the history of the Amish who live in Holmes County and the surrounding area.

BOOKSTORES

Gospel Book Store
(Located in German Village Center)
4900 Oak St., Berlin, OH 44654
330-893-2523
mygospelbookstore.com/home.asp

The Gospel Shop
112 E Main St., Sugarcreek, OH 44681
330-852-4223
gospelshopsugarcreek.com

Country Furniture and Book Store
4329 County Rd. 168, Millersburg, OH 44654
330-893-4455

SUGGESTED
ITINERARIES

FREE ACTIVITIES

AMISH COUNTRY CLASSICS

KID-FRIENDLY

OFF THE BEATEN PATH

• •

DATE NIGHT

BACKROAD ADVENTURES

HISTORY LOVERS

HISTORY LOVERS

• •

ACTIVITIES
BY SEASON

SUMMER

Enjoy Life on the Farm at Hershberger's Farm and Bakery, 30
Vote for Winning Ribs and Barbecue, 52
Putt-Putt a Hole in One, 67
Gather Fresh Produce from Roadside Stands, 114
Stop and Smell the Roses, 130

FALL

Drink Craft Beer with the Wooly Pigs, 10
Sample Sweets from Local Authentic Bakeries, 12
Laugh Until You Cry, 32
Sing with an Auctioneer, 34

WINTER

Recharge at Local Coffee Shops, 18
Bundle Up and Eat Where You Buy Your Christmas Tree, 26
Visit an "Amish Wal-Mart," 36
Celebrate Christmas Any Time of the Year, 102
Light Up Your Life with Heavenly Scents, 118

SPRING

Feed the Animals by Hand on an Amish Horse-Drawn Wagon, 39
Live like the Amish for an Afternoon, 46
Kayak and Play in the Canoe Capital of Ohio, 62
Be a Birder at Miller Manor, 71

• •

INDEX

• •

● ●

• •